AMERICAN CULTURAL HERITAGE: NAVIGATING THE FUTURE WITH THE TRUTHS OF THE PAST

Grover L. Plunkett
Faulkner University
Montgomery, Alabama

Cover design:
*Cover photo Copyright © 2019 James C. Guy

Author: Grover L. Plunkett

Printed in the United States of America

First Printing: February, 2017 (AMZ 1st edition)
Printed by Amazon's KDP printing service

ISBN-13 978-1-7976405-2-5

CONTENTS

PREFACE

At a time when so many acquire their knowledge of history from movies and social media, it is important to gain a functioning understanding of the truth of our American Heritage so that one may be able to refute and challenge those who would rewrite and re-interpret history in order to accomplish some politically correct aim. I have included numerous resources in the Bibliography section of this work so that the reader may be able to trace my efforts to facts and the truth.

I read a good book once that asserted, "You shall know the truth, and the truth shall set you free." If freedom is our aim in America and our purpose is to perpetuate it to future generations, then we must pursue the truth with great vigor in order to know it. Knowing the truth of our past truly empowers us to navigate our future. It is my hope that in some small way this work will inspire the student to pursue the truth to whatever horizon it might take.

INTRODUCTION

In Alexis de Tocqueville's book *Democracy in America*, he observes that "in the United States the sovereign authority is religious, and consequently hypocrisy must be common; but there is no country in the world where the Christian religion retains greater influence over the souls of men than in America." Does it remain so today?

- 95% of Americans claim to believe in God
- 70% say they would not vote for a presidential candidate who does not believe in God
- 70% say Jesus is the divine Son of God
- 34% claim to be born again
- Over 50% say that the Bible is the word of God and that it is true
- Six out of seven say that the Ten Commandments are relevant today
- 57% say that religion is important to their lives
- Less than half of those who believe the Ten Commandments are relevant can name four of the commandments

- What is it we are trying to learn?
    - What does religion tell us about American Culture?
    - What does American Culture tell us about American religion?
        - Has it shaped our belief system?
        - Has it affected the morality of the nation?
        - Does it affect our priorities?
        - Does it have anything to do with our world view?

- Two meanings of religion
    - Transcendent Faith ... belief in a Deity
    - One's highest commitments in life
        - Nation
        - Family
        - Political party
        - Others

- How did religion shape America from its founding?
- How did Protestant Christianity in particular shape America?
- Is there a connection between the expansion of a technological culture and the proliferation of religions and renewal of old ones?
- What does it mean to be Secular?

CHAPTER 1-

The Idea of America

Objectives
1. Explain why the truth is important in history and culture.
2. Explain why conscience motivated some who explored and settled North America.
3. List the primary nations that explored and settled North America.
4. Describe how the English system of colonization proved to be more successful.
5. Identify the elements of Colonial American life that led to a sense of independence.

America is no more than an idea, accepted by those who love her and those who believe in the idea of America. A former American president once remarked that "a people who know not from whence they came cannot know who they are or where they are bound." This could not be truer of America. This is why it is so important to grasp and understand the truth about "who" America is and "how" America arrived at this place of such influence in the world. If we are to know who we are, we must endeavor to know who we were and from whence we came.

To understand who America is, one must look at the cultural roots of America. To understand our culture, it is vital to know the origins of our people. There are very few Native Americans in the United States relative to the overall population of the nation. For this reason, we know that our culture has been dominated by those who are from some other place. At least, the roots are someplace else. Who were the earliest explorers and settlers in North America? Why did they leave Europe to come to a wilderness halfway around the world? What motivated them to leave what they knew behind to come to an unknown place? Knowing the truth about these questions will give the student of American Culture an important understanding of the complex mixture of people we call Americans.

Truth is absolute. A half-truth is as much a lie as an outright fabrication is. The truth is important in history and culture because with it we are better able to navigate the future and to understand who we are. This reality is as old as time itself. Consider this story:

Now the serpent was more crafty than any of the wild animals the Lord God had made. He said to the woman, "Did God really say, 'You must not eat from any tree in the garden?'" The woman said to the serpent, "We may eat fruit from the trees in the garden, but God did say, 'You must not eat fruit from the tree that is in the middle of the garden, and you must not touch it, or you will die.'"

"You will not certainly die," the serpent said to the woman. "For God knows that when you eat from it your eyes will be opened, and you will be like God, knowing good and evil." When the woman saw that the fruit of the tree was good for food and pleasing to the eye, and also desirable for gaining wisdom, she took some and ate it. She also gave some to her husband, who was with her, and he ate it. Then the eyes of both of them were opened, and they realized they were naked; so they sewed fig leaves together and made coverings for themselves. (Genesis 3: 1-7)

Deceived by a half truth, the woman was unable to navigate toward the future. The most tragic of the consequences is that her subsequent actions would lead to death. While a lack of understanding of our past may not lead to our demise, it makes it very difficult to navigate the future without the wisdom of the past. In this story we learn some essential *characteristics of being a human*. While one is capable of being deceived, it is less likely to occur if one knows the truth and does not stray from it. We also learn that the woman in the story knew the truth but entertained the idea that there might be something to be known beyond the truth. Knowing the truth, the woman behaves *irrationally* by eating something she knew would bring about death. Her considerations were *rational* (good for food, attractive to the eye, and desirable to gain wisdom). Her actions were *irrational* (knowing the penalty was death, ate anyway). Having eaten the fruit, she and the man were immediately stricken of *conscience* because they hid themselves from God. If only the two of them had known the painful consequences of an action that would cause conscience to condemn them even before the Lord God came calling for them. Conscience would have governed their behavior in the face of the deception they encountered.

The human being is equipped with the innate ability to know the truth when we hear it. Human behavior is governed by conscience. Whenever the human hears that which he knows or suspects to be untrue, conscience becomes the guide for action. This is the essence of rational thought. If deceived by a lie, the human may act in an irrational manner. And the consequence of such behavior is a stricken conscience. If one acts contrary to conscience long enough, and many do, the result is an irrational human being who is no longer governed by conscience.

One who is stricken of conscience cannot be happy. The recovery from such a sadness is the commitment to oneself to abandon anything that would cause one to return to this stricken state. It is what Thomas Jefferson refers to as "the pursuit of happiness;" the freedom to live as one who is free from a guilty conscience. Conscience is the greatest motivator of free men. How did conscience motivate those who would explore and settle North America?

Through sheer observation of ships approaching the port of Genoa, Christopher Columbus knew the Earth itself to be a globe. Once again, an innate ability to know the truth. The knowledge of it drove him to prove his theory to a doubting populace who believed him to be irrational. The doubters based their position upon what they believed to be established truth.

Even the future financiers of his expedition would not believe Columbus's theory until he could demonstrate that it was true. As devout Christians, Ferdinand and Isabella of Spain needed proof from the truth of the Holy Scriptures. And though it took months for Columbus to discover it, he returned with the truth: "He sits enthroned above the circle of the earth, and its people are like grasshoppers. He stretches out the heavens like a canopy, and spreads them out like a tent to live in." (Isaiah 40:22) The truth compelled Columbus and the Spanish Monarchs to go beyond what was known and to be guided into the future with the truth. Conscience would not allow the Spanish Monarchs to invest in such a strange adventure without the proof of scripture.

The Columbian Expedition would increase the wealth of Spain with gold and silver from the New World. Other treasures such as food, exotic resources, and trade made Spain the ruler of the seas for another century. Such a story should provide plenty of motivation to follow truth and conscience.

The rulers of Europe in the 16th century were considered papal princes and extensions of the power and influence of the Catholic Church and its pope. Loyalty was expected, and it was extended. However, in 1530 English King Henry VIII requested a divorce from his wife, Catherine of Aragon, in order for him to marry Anne Boleyn. His marriage to Catherine was of particular import because she was the daughter of Ferdinand and Isabella of Spain. A divorce would cause a rift in the relations between England and Spain, but Henry was determined to have his way.

When the divorce request of Henry was denied by Pope Clement VII, Henry established the Church of England and made himself the leader of that church. Henry divorced Catherine, married Anne Boleyn, and began a policy of requiring an oath of loyalty to him, acknowledging his marriage to Anne Boleyn, and recognizing the Church of England. Those who refused suffered death or severe persecution and confiscation of their property. When Henry died, his Catholic daughter from his marriage to Catherine of Aragon became queen. Queen Mary began to persecute those who had pledged loyalty to Henry and the Church of England.

When Elisabeth, Henry's daughter with Anne Boleyn, became queen, she restored the protestant faith of her father to England. Though not nearly as destructive and cruel as her half sister Mary, Elisabeth's policy still had a disruptive effect on the average citizen of England. Following her death, religious quarrels of all sorts erupted in England as to the supremacy of religion, what that religion should be, whether or not the monarch should have supreme power over the people, and to what extent the monarch's power would have in relation to the Parliament.

In 1588, the Spanish Armada sailed toward the English Channel to end any prospect that England might ally with France against them. The adventure was a cataclysmic failure. The destruction of the Spanish Armada would end Spain's domination of the seas and insure that England would emerge as the preeminent exploration and colonization power in the New World. Spain's influence would be confined to the coastal regions of the Gulf of Mexico and the eastern seaboard of present day Florida. Further, English trading companies would now flourish without the threat of Spanish pirating and the disruption of their trade.

Chartered by the various monarchs of England, English trading companies began the process of establishing trading colonies in North America in order to exploit the abundance of resources available in this untouched land. Coupled with the desire of many to leave England to practice their religious faith as they wished in North America and the English trading companies' desire for colonial trading outposts, immigration from England to North America was set to explode. The first of these colonies were in Virginia in 1607 established by the Virginia Company and in Massachusetts in 1620 at Plymouth established by the Plymouth Company.

For the settlers at Plymouth, conscience took them out of England to a place in which they could freely practice their religious faith without fear of the persecutions that had ravaged England in various ways since the death of Henry VIII. It was conscience that compelled

Isabella and Ferdinand of Spain to demand evidence of the circular shape of the earth. And it was a dependence upon the truth that gave confidence to their conscientious decisions.

Spain and England were first of many nations to explore and settle in North America. The most notable are the ones whose legacies have remained in names, religion, and culture. The Southern United States, especially the coastal regions, are dotted with cities bearing the Spanish mark of their forbears. Pensacola, Tampa, St. Augustine, Apalachicola, and Miami are among the many that display the architecture, religious faith, and names of the Spanish. England, the most prominent of the exploring nations, has its mark on the American landscape from coast to coast in language, religious faith, architecture, economics, and especially law. But others came to North America as well.

The French began their exploration in North America to establish trading posts and to spread the Catholic faith to the natives of the continent from the St. Lawrence Seaway through the Great Lakes and down the Mississippi River to the Gulf of Mexico. Detroit, Des Moines, St. Louis, Baton Rouge, New Orleans, and Biloxi bear the signs of the French who first came. Unlike England, France did not suffer the persecutions of the island nation, and in short, France was not a bad place to be in the 16th and 17th centuries. And since many of the French North American settlements were in very cold regions of the continent, it was not advantageous for the average Frenchman to leave the comforts of France to weather the difficult circumstances of North American life in a French post. Nonetheless, by 1750 France laid claim to well over a third of the present day United States' land mass. War with England and the financial difficulties brought on by the exploits of Louis VI and later Napoleon Bonaparte left France with little more than a few islands in the Caribbean and momentary control in Mexico.

Because of the size of their nations, the overwhelming power of English military might, and the inability to adequately populate their colonies, Holland and Portugal saw most of their attempts at colonization in North America consolidated into English holdings by the end of the 17th century. A few remaining signs of the attempts may be seen in lower Manhattan (Holland) and in Florida (Portuguese). While many others established temporary settlements, England, Spain, France, Holland, and Portugal are the primary nations to explore and settle in North America.

The English were most successful in establishing permanent settlements in North America because of the influence and wherewithal of the Joint Stock companies. These trading companies allowed those with limited means to come to North American colonies with little expense and to share in the prosperity of the company. Further, the religious persecutions in England, the inability of some to improve their socioeconomic condition in England, and the high demand for labor made North America a very attractive alternative to England.

From 1607 until 1754, nearly 150 years, the colonials of North America functioned without the interference or intervention of the British government. The colonies had established their own governing models based on the necessities of the individual colony (General Assemblies in New England and the House of Burgesses in Virginia), established their own treaties with the natives, organized militias for their defense against the natives, established a thriving economy and trade, and enjoyed complete religious freedom. These characteristics of the colonials created a sense of independence. Many had never seen the nation their ancestors had left to come create a new life for themselves in North America. The colonists had become Americans and embodied all the characteristics that would lead to them being called such.

Chapter 1 Sources Used

Durant, Will and Ariel. *The History of Civilization.* New York: Simon and Schuster, 1975.

Moore, James P. *One Nation Under God.* New York: Doubleday, 2005.

Philbrick, Nathaniel *Mayflower: A Story of Courage, Community, and War.* New York: Penguin Group, 2006.

Schweikart, Larry and Allen, Michael A. *A Patriot's History of the United States.* New York: Sentinel Press, 2004.

Stark, Rodney. *The Victory of Reason.* New York, 2005.

CHAPTER 2-

Reformation, Enlightenment, and the Awakening

Objectives

Equip the Student with the knowledge to:

1. **Describe** how the Reformation in England affected the migration to America.

2. **Distinguish** the differences between Puritans, Puritan Separatists, Quakers, and Catholics.

3. **Define** the Great Awakening and its effect on Colonial America.

4. **Explain** the Enlightenment principles of Nature and Reason.

5. **Name** important figures who contributed to the phenomena of the Great Awakening.

O ne who is stricken of conscience cannot be happy. When one violates their conscience purposefully, there is a period in which one must recover, pledging perhaps to themselves, "I will never do that again!" Only then may one once again enjoy a clear conscience. However, when one is compelled by governing authorities to behave in a manner that violates their conscience, that person, if they are rational, must leave or harden their conscience in order to continue their behavior.

The on again, off again Reformation movements in England from 1530 – 1688 placed the English people in difficult religious and political circumstances that required them to behave in ways that were directly in conflict with their own conscience. The roller coaster ride of Catholic monarchs followed by Protestant monarchs and then back again multiple times made life in England almost untenable for the devout Christians seeking to exercise their religious faith in harmony with their conscience. Further, non-compliance with the demands of these revolving monarchs resulted in persecutions of all sorts, torture, execution, and confiscation of their property. To escape the madness of England, many made their way to North America and the bustling new colonies stretching from present day Maine to North Florida.

There were four primary religious groups who came to North America, and each had different opinions about how to worship and conduct their lives. The groups included Puritans, Puritan Separatists, Quakers, and Catholics. Puritans believed the Anglican Church was impure and was in need of purification. To achieve this purification, they desired a return to some of the long revered traditions which had been erased from the religious practices of the Anglican Church and to move away from Catholic traditions in order to become more protestant. They advocated a greater purity of worship and doctrine and demanded both personal and collective piety of the church. Although they remained in the Church of England as they sought to purify it, other Puritan groups sought a separation from the Church of England.

Puritan Separatists separated themselves from the Church of England and created more independent strands of Puritanism, including alliances with the Scottish Presbyterian churches. It was this element of Puritanism from which came the 1620 Plymouth pilgrims. Once the Plymouth colony was established, many Puritans and Puritan Separatists came to the Massachusetts Bay colony near Plymouth.

Quakers believed one could have a direct experience of Christ without the aid of any ordained clergy. This sort of doctrine flew in the face of Catholics, Anglicans, and Puritans alike. Quakers considered themselves to be the true restoration of the Christian faith to come out of the reformation era in England, and they were strict pacifists. Because of this, the Puritans believed the Quakers to be heinous heretics. Those who came to the New England colonies were banished to areas west of the Massachusetts Bay colonies, and later under a land grant given to William Penn by Charles II of England they founded their own colony which they named Pennsylvania.

Catholics suffered great persecution in both England and the North American colonies. Stringent laws were enacted against Catholic education and Catholic religious practices. The Maryland colony became a rare colony of religious toleration in an otherwise very intolerant age. Puritans in particular demonstrated a kind of militant Protestantism in Virginia and in Massachusetts. Maryland however established religious toleration laws designed to protect all religious groups from religious persecution.

A period of religious revivalism, known as the Great Awakening, brought several waves of religious enthusiasm to the North American colonies in the 18th and 19th centuries. This increased interest in religion resulted in a great surge in evangelical church membership in the colonies and may be seen as the inspiration for several religious and social reform movements. The preaching in this period was conducted, in part, by two very important and influential evangelists: George Whitfield and Jonathan Edwards.

The preaching of Whitfield and Edwards called men and women away from the ritualistic and ceremonial elements of worship and asserted that religion must be a highly personal and spiritual conviction of personal sin and a need for redemption gained only by establishing a high standard of personal morality. Unlike the Second Great Awakening that sought out the unchurched of the population, the Great Awakening of the 18th century focused attention on the existing church membership of the colonies and called attention to their ritualistic tendencies, demanding personal piety and a renewed self-awareness of sin.

Amid these surges in religious fervor, Enlightenment philosophy began to make its mark on the American colonial culture. As was discussed in chapter one, the English Colonial System was a system of establishing settlements on behalf of the exploring nation and establishing a means of commerce. Economy was at the center of the English system. And the English system emerged from a theory of "religious capitalism" as described by Randall Collins.

Collins described "religious capitalism" as a system that arose from monastic estates of Europe during the Middle Ages. These farms put innovation to work in order to increase the productivity that would elevate them above mere subsistence farming and allow for the growth of wealth. As early as the ninth century, the Church became the primary "dynamism of the medieval economy". Because of this, the Church became the largest landowner in Europe, and its wealth surpassed that of the wealthiest kings. Some have estimated that it exceeded the wealth of all the monarchies of Europe combined.

Because of the precedent set by the Church and the success experienced by colonial settlers and investors, new ideas were generally well received as long as those ideas could be reconciled with established beliefs. The emergence of cities and their ability to spread the discussion of new ideas and new developments excited the thinking. The Enlightenment became the way of life in which the glory of God could be revealed in the discovery of God's Laws at work in the universe.

Reason, it was discovered, was the way to improve society through its application and improvement. The work of Sir Isaac Newton in physics and Nicolaus Copernicus in astronomy are just a couple of examples of the scientific work of reason in determining the mysteries hidden from man until intense observation and experimentation revealed God's Law at work. God's Law is Natural Law at work. The ability to discover the mysteries behind it was innately endowed in man because he is created in the image of the living God. Nature along with man's ability to reason and understand make for an unending search for the truth in all of God's creation.

The American Enlightenment grew out of this innovative mindset that embodied the Colonial American experience. Benjamin Franklin was perhaps the most innovative thinker in 18th century America. Among his innovations were the public library system, the American Philosophical Society, the Franklin stove, volunteer fire departments, lightning rods, the glass harmonica, and much more.

Enlightenment thinking in America was not only applied to the elements of science, but also to politics. The Divine Right of kings was the prevailing political philosophy through the 16th century. By the end of the 16th century however, new political philosophies emerged, and at least in England, they addressed the power of the monarch over the conscience of the individual. The assault on established religious beliefs at the whim of a monarch led many to consider the validity of Divine Right when it directly assaulted the conscience of man.

At the forefront of such political Enlightenment were John Locke, Thomas Hobbes, Jean-Jacque Rousseau, Adam Smith, and many others. Individualism, conscience, natural law, Nature's God, and human reason took center stage for the debate of the role of government in the lives of men. Many of the Enlightenment thinkers believed that rational man does not require government at all. They believed that the conscience of man governed his behavior. For a society of rational persons, the only need for government was to protect the rational man from the irrational man who was not governed by conscience. In their estimation, the establishment of government was a social contract between man and government, and the government was to be constrained by the consent of the participants in the social contract. Man, they believed, was born with certain liberties, and other than protecting them, these liberties were outside the jurisdiction of government. Government could extend civil rights to man but were to be hands off as it related to his liberties.

Chapter 2 Sources Used

Collins, Randall. *The Sociology of Philosophies: A Global Theory of Intellectual Change.* Cambridge: Harvard University Press, 1988.

Dickens, A.G. *The English Reformation.* University Park: Pennsylvania State University Press, 1991.

Dockes, Pierre. *Medieval Slavery and Liberation.* Chicago: University of Chicago Press, 1982.

Durant, Will and Ariel. *The History of Civilization.* New York: Simon and Schuster, 1975.

Meacham, Jon. *American Gospel.* New York: Random House, 2006.

Moore, James P. *One Nation Under God.* New York: Doubleday, 2005.

CHAPTER 3-

A Nation Is Born

Objectives

1. Describe the two earliest forms of governing models in Colonial America.
2. Define the American Idea.
3. Explain how the ancients influenced the developing and establishment for government in the United States.
4. Distinguish the difference in the Federalist and Anti-Federalist view of governing roles.

From the first arrival of settlers from England in 1607 in Jamestown and the Puritan Pilgrims of Plymouth in 1620, the English government displayed little governing effort except the appointment of colonial governors and the occasional reports of the colonial representative assemblies to Parliament. The Mayflower Compact in the Plymouth Colony and the House of Burgesses in Jamestown served as early models for the governance of the colonials. The American Colonies governed themselves through their assemblies, developed their means of commerce, established militias, and established treaty relationships with the native populations.

The French and Indian War of 1754-1763 introduced a standing British army to the colonies. Financing the war to protect its colonial interests in North America greatly strained the treasury of the British Crown. Over the course of the next twelve years directly following the war, Parliament enacted a series of bills that were designed to maintain the peace in the frontier and increase revenue through taxes to fund the British war debt.

American colonials considered themselves independent because they had been operating on their own apart from Great Britain for 150 years. Colonials believed they were being taxed unfairly and without representation in the process that levied the taxes. The final blow came when parliament closed the harbor in Boston and dissolved its governing body, replacing it with hand-picked members loyal to the British crown. The action (The Intolerable Acts) prompted a call by Massachusetts and Virginia for a Continental Congress to convene in Philadelphia in September 1774. They would begin to form the country that exists today.

The United States of America is an idea. Nothing more. It is the conviction that with hard work and determination in a land of liberty, one can improve his socio-economic circumstance. There are no ethnic Americans. Americans are those who embrace the idea of America. The founders conceived of what America would be by exploring the various governments from ancient history and discarding the obvious failures while embracing the values that had succeeded in these same governments. The men that framed the government in its infancy were trained to read and to comprehend Latin and Greek so as to be able to read the ancient writings in their original form. In this way they were able to absorb lessons of leadership, valor, and governance from original, first hand witnesses to ancient governing principles. There has not been a more extraordinary group of men assembled in government since the original founders assembled to craft a system with a blank page before them.

The Greek and Roman historians and orators whom the founding fathers studied were a small select who possessed backgrounds and concerns that were similar to those of the founders themselves. Like the founders, these historians tended to be learned, moralistic, aristocratic males who possessed some political and military experience. They drew their ideas from at least ten ancient scholars and historians.

The founders differed from most of the Greeks and Romans in that they designed a government that virtually insured the extinction of their strata and the opportunity to learn from the American government. Democracy by its nature and definition insured rule by the people, and the people in large part were common, not aristocratic. Republicanism by its nature and definition insured the investment of the power of the people into a representative that spoke on their behalf. These founders of the American Republic relied heavily on the ancient writers, for in their work the founders saw truth, wisdom, and virtue that they felt to be absolute. And in the confidence of their understanding of the virtues they espoused, they formed the American government.

Lesson Learned from the Spartans in the Writings of Plutarch

The founders discovered that the degree to which republics were successful could be seen in the extent to which the collective good could be emphasized freely by the citizenry over their own individual rights when the good of the republic required it. Because of this, the founders built their republic on the natural rights of man and urged them to sacrifice for the common good. And they appreciated the stability and security gained from warfare but desired individual freedom to the extent that they rejected an exact Spartan model for the American republic.

Lessons from the Persians in the Writings of Herodotus

It is possible for a collection of small republics to defeat a centralized monarchical power in a war for survival. Because of this, free men fight better than slaves and are motivated by desire rather than fear. Further, militias composed of common citizens, motivated by love of liberty, are superior to professional armies of despotic monarchs.

Lessons from the Athenians—Thucydides

Simple democracy leads to disastrous defeat because of the natural inclination to individuality. Democracy is chronically unstable and is a society controlled by the violent, erratic tyranny of the majority. All power then must not be concentrated in the masses but must be balanced by a strong executive and powerful senate.

Lessons from Greece—Polybius and Demosthenes

It is necessary that there be a strong central government to bind together individual republics in union. Constant internal strife will lead to vulnerability to foreigners. However, strong central government is more important in times of crisis than in times of peace. Strong central government stifles individual innovation and progress and is to be viewed with skepticism.

Lessons from Rome—Cicero, Sallust, Livy, and Suetonius

Give the masses enough power to avoid a tyrannical oligarchy without giving them so much control as to establish a chaotic ochlocracy. Virtue is vital to the survival of a republic.

Lessons from the Fall of Rome—Plutarch and Sallust

Vigilance must be maintained against ambitious individuals who might threaten the republic. A republic must continually encourage the patriotic spirit of self-sacrifice.

Lessons from the Roman Emperors—Suetonius and Tacitus

Liberty is precious. Tyranny is the worst fate, for it not only deprives one of liberty, but it also deprives one of virtue.

In possession of this ancient wisdom, the great debate in the early foundation of the American government was between those that believed the nation would be best served by a strong federal government (federalists) and those who believed more power should be vested in the states and the people (anti-federalists). Both schools of thought took their position based on the writings of the ancients and the more contemporary writers of the Enlightenment.

Benjamin Rush, one of the attendees to the Constitutional Convention noted that the new government must be one "which unites with the vigor of monarchy and the stability of aristocracy with all the freedom of a simple democracy." And that, simply stated, was the challenge of the convention. Thomas Jefferson, an anti-federalist, had studied the great authors and philosophers, ancient and contemporary, for years. He considered his books to be the "mental furnishings" of his life. He loved the pursuit of knowledge and read all so that he might be equipped to argue both sides of any political debate. A student of John Locke, James Madison, also took an anti-federalist stand.

John Adams, a federalist, studied at length the orations of Cicero. He insisted that a strong central government was the best way to avoid the anarchy and chaos that might arise out of a democracy vesting too much power in the masses. Voicing a similar opinion, Alexander Hamilton, a student of the writings of Hobbes, Montaigne, and Bacon, desired a strong central government even to the extent of an elected monarchy.

The substance of the anti-federalists' debate had its foundation in Enlightenment conceptions of natural law, nature's God, and the nature of man. According to Enlightenment philosophers like John Locke and Jean-Jacque Rousseau, if man in a natural state was controlled by natural law, his conscience would dictate his behavior. In essence, the nature of man would be rational and good. A society made up of individuals such as these needs little or no governance because they would be governed by their conscience.

On the other hand, philosophers like Thomas Hobbes believed that man in a state of nature would be more inclined to animal instincts that natural law. This man would be in a war against all for survival and would be violent, brutish, and selfish. A society composed of such a populace would require a strong monarch and a powerful central government to maintain order.

In the final composition of American government, the founders compromised as to their understanding of the nature of man and formed a government that preserved the liberties of the rational man and guarded his person and interests against both irrational man and irrational government. Further, these Constitutional craftsmen formed a government that was protected against itself. Balance of power, separation of power, and federalism found a place in the construction of the new nation. Testing this governmental construct and the avenue in which to change it has become the hallmark of their genius, and longevity of the government has become a testament to the rational society which enjoys the liberties it affords.

Chapter 3 Sources Used

Ackerman, Bruce. *The Failure of the Founding Fathers.* Cambridge: Harvard University Press, 2005.

Boyer, Paul S., ed. *The Oxford Companion to United States History.* New York: Oxford University Press, 2001.

Brodie, Fawn M. *Thomas Jefferson: An Intimate History.* New York: W.W. Norton, 1974.

Burns, Eric *Infamous Scribblers.* New York: Perseus Books Group, 2006.

Calloway, Colin G. *The Scratch of a Pen 1763 and the Transformation of North America.* Oxford: Oxford University Press, 2006.

Divine, Robert A., et al. *America, Past and Present.* New York: Harper Collins, 1994.

Hamilton, Alexander, et al. *The Federalist Papers.* New York: Literary Classics, 1994.

Richard, Carl J. *Greeks, Romans, Bearing Gifts: How the Ancients Inspired the Founding Fathers.* Lanham: Bowman and Littlefield Publishers, 2008.

Schweikert, Larry, and Allen, Michael A. *A Patriot's History of the United States.* New York: Sentinel Press, 2004.

Stark, Rodney. *The Victory of Reason.* New York: Random House, 2005.

Tindall, George Brown, and Shi, David Emory. *America: A Narrative History*, 7th Ed. New York: W.W. Norton and Company, 2007.

Tocqueville, Alexis de. *Democracy in America.* London: The Folio Society, 2001.

Washington, George. *Selected Writings.* New York: Literary Classics, 1997.

Wood, Gordon S. *Revolutionary Characters: What Made the Founders Different?* New York: Penguin Group, 2006.

CHAPTER 4-

Utopian and Transcendental Thought, The Second Awakening, and American Social Movements

Objectives
1. Know the origin of Utopian thought.
2. Explain how Utopianism and Transcendentalism are related.
3. Describe the legacies of the Utopian and Transcendentalist.
4. Describe the Second Great Awakening and its effect on American culture
5. Name the three major Social Movements the emerged from the Second Great Awakening.

Utopianism has its roots in the 16th Century writings of Sir Thomas More. More originally wrote his *Utopia* for amusement. It was printed and distributed all over Europe in Latin but not printed in England until after his death. Utopia, in the imagination of More, was a mythical place, an island discovered by Raphael Hythlodaye while voyaging with Amerigo Vespucci in 1504. More described the island this way:

Among the Utopians all things being common, every man hath abundance of everything. I compare with them so many nations where every man calleth that, which he hath gotten, his own proper and private goods. I hold well with Plato that all men should have and enjoy equal portions of wealth and commodities. For where every man, under certain titles and pretenses, draweth and lucketh to himself as much as he can, so that a few will divide among themselves all the whole riches there to the residue is left lack and poverty.

One will discover in later chapters of this book how Karl Marx found a foundation for his communistic utopian ideas. To More though, this was a simple exercise in personal amusement, not a prelude to the perversions of the mind and the scarring of society.

American utopian roots may be found in 1774 and the teachings of Ann Lee. Lee was the first of Utopia seekers in the United States. She came to America from England in that year with a number of her followers. She believed God was genderless and that she was the female form of God. Her message was the pursuit of perfection in a physical existence, and she believed that celibacy prepared one for the perfection promised by heaven.

This group often experienced vision moments. On these occasions, they asserted that they received visions from heaven and prophesies. When these things occurred, they manifested themselves in emotional fits and prophesying. Because of these expressions, they became known as Shakers.

After Lee's death in 1784 the group began to spread to other parts of New England, Ohio, and Kentucky. By 1830 there were about twenty flourishing Shaker communes established. Inside these communities, all property was held in common, strict celibacy was practiced, and men and women worked, ate, and slept separately. Because of the strict celibacy practiced by these communities, there was no increase in their numbers except through conversions to the Shaker faith. With no population growth, the communities began to diminish by 1860, and over time disappeared.

The lasting legacy of the Shakers was their attention to simple beauty. From the architecture of their buildings and homes to the furniture produced by their many craftsmen, their devotion to simplicity and practicality is evident. Shaker furniture today is highly valued and much sought after.

A radical sort of Utopianism emerged in three communes, founded by three different Shaker men devoted to the common ownership of property similar to the communes established by Ann Lee. These differed though from the Lee Shakers, in that they did not practice celibacy.

The New Harmony commune was founded by Robert Owen, who actually purchased slaves to work alongside the community to accomplish the establishment of the commune. After the communes were established, the slaves were released to freedom. The Nasoba Commune was established by Frances Wright, a friend of Robert Owen. Wright's commune also purchased slaves in a practice he described as "rational cooperation." The slaves in this commune were freed after they had earned their freedom through their work. Both the Nasoba and New Harmony communes failed, suggesting that utopian socialism did not take root easily in American soil.

The Oneida commune was established by John Humphrey Noyes and initially was very successful. They, however, practiced a radical and unorthodox Christian perfectionism. Noyes taught that the second coming of Christ had already occurred and that Christians were no longer bound by the moral rules that had bound man in his previous fallen state. Traditional marriage was outlawed in the commune, and all men and women in the community were married to each other. As one might imagine, disease and jealousies were the undoing of the Oneida commune.

Seeking perfection on earth in a physical state is impossible, as evidenced by the Utopia seekers. However, there were those who believed that perfection could be attained in a spiritual or mental state. These men and women were called Transcendentalists. They emerged from a literary and philosophical movement and believed that the individual could transcend material reality and ordinary understanding and attain a higher form of reason and oneness with the universe and the spiritual forces that lay behind it.

Ralph Waldo Emerson, Henry David Thoreau, Edgar Allen Poe, and George Ripley are among some of the more notable transcendentalists of that era. Emerson was an essayist and lecturer. Perhaps one of his best works was *Self Reliance.* From it comes some of the most quoted lines used to inspire others, and it reflects the transcendentalist spirit.

"The purpose of life is not to be happy. It is to be useful, to be honorable, to be compassionate, to have it make some difference that you have lived and lived well."

"Dare to live the life you have dreamed for yourself. Go forward and make your dreams come true."

"Don't choose the better person, choose the person who makes a better you."

Thoreau's words similarly inspire:

"It's the beauty within us that makes it possible for us to recognize the beauty around us. The question is not what you look at but what you see."

"Most men lead lives of quiet desperation and go to the grave with the song still in them."

"If a man does not keep pace with his companions, perhaps it is because he hears a different drummer. Let him step to the music which he hears, however measured or far away."

And Edgar Allen Poe:

"Yes, I now feel that it was then on that evening of sweet dreams- that the very first dawn of human love burst upon the icy night of my spirit. Since that period I have never seen nor heard your name without a shiver half of delight, half of anxiety."

The lasting legacy of the transcendentalists may be seen in these inspirational words and in them one may get a glimpse of their concept for mental and spiritual perfection. Their writing calls one to see the world differently and to see it in its best form. All three of the above mentioned men sought that sort of perfection. Poe claimed to not like transcendentalists. And his work may well be considered a part of romanticism. Yet to the reader of his work, some of his themes are very much akin to the work of other transcendentalists.

The Second Great Awakening was a period of spiritual revival in America and included both the fiery sermons of the revivalists and the intertwining of the political and social conditions of the country with Christian doctrines and social norms. These "camp meetings," as they were often called, brought people together for rare social interactions with far away neighbors and gave them the inspiration they needed for change to important social issues. Perhaps the three most important social movements to emerge from the Second Great Awakening were abolitionism, temperance, and women's suffrage.

Abolition was nothing new to the conversation of Americans in the early 19th century. The practice of slavery seemed a paradox in a land of liberty that espoused such lofty aims as "all men created equal" and "life, liberty and the pursuit of happiness." How to end slavery became the theme discussed amongst those in the abolitionist movement. From theme's indecisive perspective emerged three approaches to the question of slavery.

Some abolitionists were gradualists. This group believed slaves' freedom should be purchased, and those freed slaves be sent back to Africa to a colony established especially for freed slaves.

Others were considered radical abolitionists. This group believed that slavery should be ended by inciting a slave revolt and bringing slavery to an end by force, even if it meant overthrowing the government of the United States. Among these were John Brown and his followers. We will consider more about Brown in the next chapter.

Finally, the remaining group were simply referred to as abolitionists. This group sought a legal and political end to slavery through petition, referendum, and electing abolitionists to high office. They believed with the right political climate, the right people in office, and the opportune event, slavery could be brought to an end.

Chapter 4 Sources Used

Borneman, Walter R. *1812: The War that Forged a Nation.* New York: Harper Collins, 2004.

Boyer, Paul S., ed. *The Oxford Companion to United States History.* New York: Oxford University Press, 2001.

Cheek, H. Lee, Jr. *John C. Calhoun: Selected Writings and Speeches.* Washington, D.C.: Regnery Publishing, 2003.

Divine, Robert A., et al. *America, Past and Present.* New York: Harper Collins, 1994.

Durant, Will and Ariel. *The History of Civilization.* New York: Simon and Schuster, 1975.

Filler, Louis. *The Crusade Against Slavery.* New York: Harper and Row, 1960.

Howe, Daniel Walker. *What God Hath Wrought.* New York: Oxford University Press, 2007.

McDougall, Walter A. *Throes of Democracy.* New York: Harper and Collins, 2008.

Meacham, Jon. *American Gospel.* New York: Random House, 2006.

Moore, James P. *One Nation Under God.* New York: Doubleday, 2005.

Pease, William H. and Jane H. *The Anti-Slavery Argument.* New York: Bobbs-Merrill, 1965.

Schweikert, Larry and Allen, Michael A. *A Patriot's History of the United States.* New York: Sentinel Press, 2004.

Stark, Rodney. *The Victory of Reason.* New York: Random House, 2005.

Taylor, William R. *Cavalier and Yankee, The Old South and the American National Character.* New York: Harper and Row, 1969.

Tindall, George Brown, and Shi, David Emory *America: A Narrative History,* 7th ed. New York: W.W. Norton, 2007.

CHAPTER 5-

The Advent of War, The War Between the States, and The Reconstruction

Objectives

Equip the student with the knowledge to:

\# 1. Explain the complex array of social and political issues at work in Advent of War.

\# 2. Describe the two great compromises made by Congress regarding the admission of states.

\# 3. Know the differences in Nationalism and Sectionalism.

\# 4. Identify the work of the Temperance Movement, The American Colonization Society, and the Abolition Movement.

\# 5. Describe the Secession Differences in the Deep South and the Upper South

\# 6. Explain what Reconstruction meant to the South.

\# 7. Explain the significance of the Hayes/Tilden Presidential Election to the South and Reconstruction

\# 8. Explain the lasting resentments in the South following Reconstruction.

The paradox mentioned in the previous chapter plagued the American mind from the very inception of the nation. It had been wrestled with in the Constitutional Convention, but the issue was pushed further down the road to be dealt with. The arguments included how to count slaves in a national census, if slaves should be considered in the apportionment of representation in Congress, should slaves be considered citizens of the United States, and whether it was moral for the institution of slavery to even exist in a nation founded on liberty.

Article I, Section 9 of the Constitutions of the United States asserts, "The migration or importation of such persons as any of the states now existing shall think proper to admit, shall not be prohibited by the Congress prior to the year one thousand eight hundred and eight, but a tax or duty may be imposed on such importation, not exceeding ten dollars for each person."

The article was placed in the Constitution to stop the importation of slaves into the United States by 1808. It did end the legal importation as such, but the smuggling of slaves into the United States continued for some time. The founding fathers had built in the article to begin the reform of an institution that was intertwined with the political, economic, and social way of life in the United States. Slavery stood in stark contrast to the words of the Declaration of Independence—"Life, Liberty and the Pursuit of Happiness." But slavery was only part of the complex mixture of issues and values that would tear the country apart by the end of 1865.

From the ratification of the Constitution in 1787 until the Election of 1860, the Congress had found a way to compromise on the most divisive issues as a result of the efforts of John C. Calhoun, Daniel Webster, and Henry Clay. As these voices grew faint in Congress, compromise became all but impossible. The nation was torn apart by several issues.

Slavery presented an interesting debacle for those who wished to attack it on moral grounds. The anti-slavery element of the Constitutional Convention believed the institution should end, but to do so would present the dilemma of citizenship. Would freed slaves be given the right of citizenship, and if citizenship, then the right to vote? Counting slaves as a part of the overall population, in the estimation of northern states, would give the southern states too much power in the federal Congress. And yet their push to end slavery would bring the power they were so determined to minimize. The compromise was to count the slave population as only 3/5 of a person. In this way, deference would be made to the actual numbers without giving too much power to slave states in the South. Further, it was hoped that the 1808 Prohibition Clause would diminish the slave trade and slavery altogether.

Missouri's petition to be admitted to the Union in 1820 as a slave state presented Congress with its first real test of the viability of the compromises of 1787. With Missouri becoming a slave state the balance of power in Congress would be altered and a compromise had to be reached. A student of history should note that the greatest outcry over Missouri's admission was the power imbalance, not the slave state issue. The Missouri Compromise allowed Missouri's admission as a slave state and divided Massachusetts into two states making Maine the balancing free state admission. Also, the southern border of Missouri became the northernmost boundary for admission of any new slave states.

A few years later in 1839, the Spanish slave ship *Amistad* was taken into custody by the United States Navy. After boarding the ship, naval officers discovered that the slaves that were being transported to the United States had taken over the ship and killed all but two of its original crew. The slaves were placed in a Connecticut jail and tried for murder. Defense attorneys demonstrated that the Africans on board were being illegally smuggled into the United States in violation of the 1808 Prohibition Clause in the Constitution. The lower court verdict was challenged in the United States Supreme Court.

The case was presented in the Supreme Court by former President of the United States John Quincy Adams. Adams' appeal to the court was to uphold the ideals of freedom which the United States promoted abroad. The Supreme Court ruled in favor of the Africans because they had been born in Africa and kidnapped from there, and they were to be freed and returned to Africa. The verdict sent shock ways through Spain because Spain claimed the ship, and its cargo belonged to Spain. Slave interests in the South feared the ruling would incite anti-slave rebellion and pit the nation against their interests.

The balance in Congress was threatened again when Texas won its independence from Mexico in March 1836. Immediately the Texans petitioned for admission into the Union as a slave state. It would not be until 1845 that Texas would finally be admitted as a slave state, when Iowa was admitted as a free state. Once again the balance of power was maintained in Congress between slave and free state, but not permanently.

The discovery of gold in California in 1849 created a population explosion in that territory and led to California's petition to be admitted to the Union in 1850. With no slave state under consideration for admission, a compromise was necessary. The Compromise of 1850 would be the last congressional compromise before the nation lurched into war, and it is likely that the compromise itself led to the War Between the States. Under the compromise:

1. California was admitted as a free state.
2. A Fugitive Slave Act was passed to allow slave owners to retrieve their slaves even if they had fled to a free state.
3. The Utah Territory was established.
4. The New Mexico Territory was established, and the Western boundary of Texas was set.
5. Slave trade in Washington, D.C. was prohibited.

In 1852, Harriett Beecher Stowe's *Uncle Tom's Cabin* was published and presented to an uninformed public the horrors of slavery, as well as the familial relationship that often developed between master and slave. The public grasped hold of the tragic ending of the novel, and it fostered an increased animosity toward the institution of slavery and the South in general. It is said that upon meeting Ms. Stowe, President Lincoln said, "so you're the little lady that started this big war!" Clearly the publishing of the novel invigorated abolitionists and informed the public of the slave's life. Many believe it contributed to the multiple causes of the War Between the States.

To further agitate anti-slave elements against the slave interests of the South, the Dred Scott decision by the Supreme Court in 1857 put more fuel to the fire of abolitionism. Dred Scott had been a slave all his life but had been sold to a federal army office who took him to free states and territories. When his master died and he became the property of the master's widow, Dred Scott sued for his freedom. Had he petitioned the State of Louisiana for his freedom it would most likely would have granted his request. Instead, Scott sued in district court and appealed all the way to the Supreme Court. In its landmark ruling, the Supreme Court ruled that since Scott was a slave, he was not a citizen (an issue that dates back to the arguments of the Constitutional Convention) and had no standing in the court and was remanded back into slavery.

The 1854 Kansas-Nebraska Act created a slave issue controversy that resulted in some of the most violent encounters in Kansas history. The act in many ways was an attempt at compromise between those who desired a Northern route for the Transcontinental Railroad and slave interests seeking new lands in the West. In exchange for consideration for the Northern railroad route, railroad interests agreed to a popular sovereignty approach to the issue of slavery, allowing each state to determine their status in the crafting of their own constitutions. The act effectively repealed the Missouri Compromise and left slavery open to the vote of the people in each state. So violent were anti-slavery forces against slave interests that Kansas became known as "Bleeding Kansas."

Contributing to the nickname was radical abolitionist John Brown. Brown and his followers went to Kansas to insure that Kansas became a free state by whatever means necessary.

He and his men attacked a group of pro-slavery settlers near Pottawatomie, Kansas in 1856 and murdered five men there before fleeing. His radical intentions would be further manifested in his attempt to take control of the federal arsenal at Harper's Ferry, Virginia two years later.

Nationalism is a desire to do that which is best for one's nation and evokes a great sense of pride in the culture and social dynamic of one's nation. It is one of the considerations the founders noted when reading the political writings of the ancients. Sallust had written of the Roman republic and its fall to despotic imperialism that "a republic must continually encourage a patriotic spirit of self-sacrifice." But the actions of government in the days leading to the War Between the States increasing led the nation to Sectionalism. Sectionalism is a desire to elevate one's section of the country above the collective well-being of the nation. It embodies the same pride in culture and social dynamic, but excludes and fails to consider the rest of the nation.

Concurrent with the slave issue and the continued struggle for sectional power in the federal Congress was the ever increasing tariff burden that was being placed unevenly upon the Southern states. With peace restored between the United States and Great Britain following the War of 1812, Great Britain flooded the United States markets with cheap imports. American industrial interests, located predominantly in the Northern states, demanded protection from these imports with tariffs. The Tariff of 1816 was initially intended to protect American businesses rather than generate revenues for the government. Because the tariff was to protect manufacturers, and there were more factories in the North as opposed to the South, the tariff became a sectional issue. To exacerbate the tariff issue, the funds were spent mainly on internal improvements. These improvements included railroads, roads, and canals that were being constructed mainly in areas that benefitted the Northern states.

By 1860, 87% of all revenues flowing into the Federal Treasury were being paid by the states that would eventually make up the Confederate States of America. Of that 87%, nearly 95% of that total was coming from the state of South Carolina alone. South Carolina had long resisted the constant increase in tariffs, and its congressional delegation paid close attention to the political leanings of the upcoming Presidential election.

Whigs made up the majority of congressmen who desired taxes. One Whig, Abraham Lincoln, was a strong supporter of tariffs. Though the Whigs performed well in the South in each election cycle, their position on tariffs was a source of discontent toward them from Southerners. Lincoln often said in his campaign addresses, "My platform is short and sweet, like a widow's dance. More tariffs and more internal improvements." As a Presidential candidate, he posed a real threat to South Carolinians. His election in 1860 was all South Carolina could bear. Knowing Lincoln would raise tariffs that were already burdensome to South Carolina, the state seceded only six weeks after Lincoln's election. By February 1861, six more Southern states had seceded. In convention in Montgomery, Alabama, the seceded states adopted a Constitution of the Confederate States of America and elected Senator Jefferson Davis of Mississippi as its President.

In Lincoln's inaugural address he revealed his lack of understanding of the issue behind South Carolina's secession and those states that had followed her. South Carolina, like her revolutionary forefathers, was "dissolving the bands that had connected them to another" because of oppressive taxation with no hope they would cease to increase any time soon thereafter. But instead of focusing on the issue of the tariffs, Lincoln's address declares that he has no intention of bringing an end to slavery. Instead, Lincoln and others supported the Corwin Amendment that would perpetuate the legality of slavery forever. And he also made it clear that he must save the Union.

March 2, 1861, the U.S. Congress passed the Corwin Amendment, which guaranteed permanent slavery in the U.S., after most Southern States had withdrawn from the (then) voluntary Union. It was ratified by three Northern States: Ohio, Maryland and Illinois but by none of the Southern States. On the very same day, Congress also passed the Morrill Tariff Act, (U.S. Statutes At Large 36th Congress, Session 2, Chapter 68), which raised the Federal sales tax on imports from an average 20% to an average 40%. This then allowed Northern manufacturers to raise their prices 40% higher than prices were for European imports with no tariff. It is clear now that the federal government sought to placate Southern interests by perpetuating slavery while failing to understand that slavery was not the issue at all. It was the ever increasing taxes.

March 4, 1861, Lincoln stated in his First Inaugural Address:

"The power confided to me will be used to hold, occupy, and possess the property and places belonging to the government (four Federal tax collection forts including Fort Sumter), and to collect the duties and imposts (import tax); but beyond what may be necessary for these objects, there will be no invasion, no using of force against or among the people anywhere. I have no purpose, directly or indirectly, to interfere with the institution of slavery in the States where it exists. I believe I have no lawful right to do so, and I have no inclination to do so. I understand a proposed (Corwin) Amendment to the Constitution has passed Congress, to the effect that the Federal Government shall never interfere with the domestic institutions of the States, including that of persons held to service. Holding such a provision to now be implied constitutional law, I have no objection to its being made express and irrevocable."

While Lincoln was maneuvering to save the union by perpetuating slavery, South Carolina and the Confederacy were moving to evict federal forces from Fort Sumter in South Carolina's Charleston Bay. Removing federal forces from South Carolinian property would end the federal collection of taxes in the harbor. Further, it would put the federal government in a position of having to find revenues for operations elsewhere.

With a delegation from the Confederate states waiting for an audience with Lincoln to discuss the peaceful solution to the impending crisis, both Lincoln and Secretary of State William Seward delayed. Seward continued to promise the Southern delegation that preparations were being made to evacuate Fort Sumter as Lincoln delayed discussions. Observers in Charleston saw no indication that preparations were being made to evacuate Sumter. Not until April 8, 1861, was the Southern delegation notified that the federal forces at Fort Sumter would not leave. In fact, a ship had already sailed to resupply and reinforce Fort Sumter. Honest Abe indeed!

In spite of the lies and delays Southern peace delegates were subjected to, they continuously repeated their demands that the federal command evacuate and abandon Fort Sumter so the crisis could be resolved peacefully. No civilized nation, seeking to maintain its national honor would have considered such a ruse as anything other than an act of war. With peaceful efforts snubbed, Confederate forces opened fire on the fortress at 4:30 am April 12, 1861. A day later federal forces surrendered the fortress and effectively brought an end to the collection of federal taxes in South Carolina. The loss of Fort Sumter and the federal taxes that were imposed in Charleston Harbor was a defeat Lincoln could not bear. It was this loss that made clear Lincoln's motives for saving the union. In his April 15th War Proclamation, Lincoln never mentions slavery. His focus was tax revenue, but he believed Southern motivation was slavery:

Whereas, the (revenue) laws of the United States have been for some time past, and now are opposed by combinations too powerful to be suppressed by the ordinary course, now, therefore, I call forth the militia of the several States, to the aggregate number of 75,000, in order to suppress said combinations, and to cause the laws to be duly executed.

And again on April 19:

Whereas an insurrection against the Government of the United States has broken out and the laws of the United States for the collection of the revenue cannot be effectually executed therein: Now, therefore, I have further deemed it advisable to set on foot a blockade of the ports within the States aforesaid.

With the April 19 proclamation, Lincoln committed an act of war against Great Britain. As an island nation, Great Britain was and continues to be a nation that is dependent upon imported goods and resources for the sustainability of its economy.

Any threat to this flow of trade to the British is tantamount to an act of war. The proclamation was a direct affront to the British trade policy and was a puzzling act in light of the lofty esteem Americans declared to have for liberty and independence. These Southern states to which Lincoln's proclamation was addressed were demanding independence, and Lincoln was closing the ports in order to collect taxes. To the British, this was a reminder of the similar action taken by the British against its colonies some eighty years earlier. According to Arnstein, "British recognition of Southern belligerency in May 1861...merely took cognizance of a state of affairs that Lincoln himself had previously acknowledged in proclaiming a blockade of the Southern ports". To the British, this act and the subsequent Trent Affair were an affront to British neutrality and a violation of the freedom of the seas. More importantly, these acts became a roadblock to the British quest for globalism, not an offense to the British view on slavery.

When considered in context of the passage of the Corwin Amendment in Congress, both Congress and President Lincoln believed that Southern slaveholding interests would be willing to pay higher taxes if the institution of slavery were perpetuated. But South Carolina had made her intentions clear from the beginning. On December 25, 1860, South Carolina declared unfair taxes as a cause of secession in her *Address of South Carolina to Slaveholding States*:

The British parliament undertook to tax the Colonies, to promote British interests. Between taxation without any representation, and taxation without a representation adequate to protection, there was no difference. And so with the Southern States towards the Northern States, in the vital matter of taxation, they are in a minority in Congress. The people of the Southern States are not only taxed for the benefit of the Northern States, but after the taxes are collected, three-fourths (75%) of them are expended at the North.

In the estimation of Lt. Colonel Robert E. Lee, Lincoln's call for 75,000 troops to put down the rebellion in the "cotton states," "did nothing to ameliorate the crisis. It has only deepened it. For by calling up 75,000 troops he has made his enemy the state directly across the Potomac River!" Within weeks of making his Proclamation of War, the Upper South states of Virginia, North Carolina, Tennessee, and Arkansas had seceded, and articles of secession were being proposed in Missouri, Kentucky,

Maryland, and Delaware. While the Lower South states had seceded in large part because of intolerable taxation, the Upper South seceded because they were being invaded by the federal government they had created. In the words of President Jefferson Davis, "This is the lamentable and fundamental error on which rests the policy that has culminated in his declaration of War against these Confederate States. An organization (Union) created by the States to secure the blessings of liberty and independence against foreign aggression, has been gradually perverted into a machine for their (the States) control. The creature (federal government) has been exalted above its creators (the States)." On the day Robert E. Lee was offered command of the federal forces to put down the rebellion, an offer he refused, he lamented, "I never thought I would see a day arrive when a President of the United States would raise an army to invade his own country!"

The War Between the States is often called the Second American Revolution because it has so many parallel issues. First, two very distinct different worldviews formed in distinctly different geographical areas, and the issues separating them became completely irreconcilable.

Second, the primary focus of the dispute was centered on taxes, the unfairness of taxes, and the proper collection and distribution of the taxes collected. And third, the concentration of power and the unwillingness to share it or give it up. In the end, the tragedy occurred because of an inability to compromise.

By the end of 1865, 25% of the population living in the South prior to the War Between the States were dead from war, disease, malnutrition, or exposure. The smell of death hung in the air for five years following the war. Food shortages became chronic contributors to crime and violence. Frederick Douglass lamented the plight of the freed slave: "He has neither money, property, nor friends. He is free from the old plantation, but now has nothing but the dusty road under his feet. He has been turned loose, naked, hungry, and destitute to the open sky."

Only days after the war ended, John Wilkes Booth, envisioning himself as a modern day Brutus saving his republic from the designs of a despotic tyrant, shot President Lincoln as he sat watching a play in Washington's Ford Theatre. It was a stunning and bold action, but Lincoln's sudden death elevated him to the level of a deity in the North. The President who stumbled into an all-out rebellion, misunderstood the intentions of the South, cost the lives of hundreds of thousands, inculcated a hatred and resentment between races and sections of the country, who vowed on numerous occasions to perpetuate slavery, and brought the United States to the brink of war with both Great Britain and France, would be lauded as the "Great Emancipator" and the greatest President to ever govern the United States.

As for the South in general, the former Confederate States were placed under military control, divided into military districts, and governed by federal Army generals. A plan of reconstruction was debated in Congress and finally passed, which subjugated the Southern people to such injustice, brutality, and incivility that the resentments associated with that time would live up until this very day. No term in modern history so poorly describes a period of time in history as does the term Reconstruction. Reconstruction is more appropriately used as a descriptor of a period of history rather than any reconstructing activities that took place in the South between 1865 and 1877. The motto of the average Southerner became "Never Again!

Never again will we be oppressed beneath the boot of a federal tyrant."

The Freedmen's Bureau was organized by Congress to "relieve the suffering of the destitute refugees, freedmen, and their wives and children." But the agency was rife with corruption and unfair practices. Consequently, very little temporary relief was provided, and constitutional rights and legal rights were reserved only for freedmen. To further exacerbate the suffering of the Southern people, including freed slaves, men from the North descended upon the desperate populace and took advantage of their plight by seizing property for the taxes imposed against the property owners, transacting unscrupulous contracts, and threatening all with violence. This group of Northern charlatans, known to Southerners as Carpetbaggers, were in league with other Southerners who sought to take advantage of the desperate populace. This group of Southerners became known as scalawags.

Congress busied itself with the task of destroying the democrat party and breaking the political hold that prominent Southern planters held within that party. The first order of business was the issue of slavery. The 13th amendment abolishing slavery insured that the property rights planters had in slaves was removed and their source of cheap labor ended. But by ending slavery, Northern members of congress found themselves in a dilemma that plagued them from the inception of the republic. By virtue of their freedom, slaves were entitled to citizenship, but citizenship would also swing the power of the populace's proportional representation in congress to the South. In order to minimize the effect of such a situation, the 14th amendment, giving the right of citizenship to former slaves, also included an *ex post facto* law. This law disenfranchised anyone who aided or participated in the Confederate cause. This effectively disenfranchised the white Southern voting populace and made certain the Radical Republican elements in the Congress could control the electoral affairs of the several states of the old Confederacy. Southern states that had been readmitted to the Union were forced out of the Union, and the ratification of the 14th amendment was made a condition for readmission. Closely associated with the 14th amendment, the final blow to Southern "home rule" was the 15th amendment, which gave voting rights to former male slaves. This insured that Southern congressional delegations would be, for the most part, black.

Other indignities were imposed on Southerners, such as the demand that each major city in the South rename one street in their city "Union Street." Throughout the South today, one is reminded of this imposition on the people of those cities. The song Dixie was outlawed in many areas. Even the whistling of the tune was forbidden. In passive resistance to the humiliations imposed by this occupying force, spittoons and chamber pot manufacturers began to emblazon the bottoms of those vessels with the likenesses of Lincoln, Benjamin "The Beast" Butler, and William T. Sherman. To the Southerner, it seemed to have made the use of both more enjoyable!

The Election of 1876 was a turning point for the South. Rutherford B. Hayes and Samuel Tilden tied for the electoral vote for the presidency. The tie seemed impossible to break until Hayes convinced Southern delegations to vote for him in exchange for removing federal troops from the South. Of course, these delegations jumped at the chance. Hayes was elected President, federal troops were removed from the South, and "home rule" was again restored to Southern states. Reconstruction had finally ended and the "great nightmare" was over.

Southerners still seethed with resentments from the injustices perpetrated during the Reconstruction. Home rule meant returning power back to old power brokers in agriculture along with new ones in industry and finance. Southern legislatures began the task of initiating policies that insured the "never again" motto carried weight.

Jim Crow laws were laws put in place to maximize the power of the white voting populace, minimize the power of the black voting populace, and prevent the possibility that the power gained would never be reversed. Among the laws instituted were poll tax laws and poll test laws. Both were used to advantage white voters over black voters.

Property tax laws in the South have their origins in the agricultural nature of the post war Southern economy. Because cotton was the cash crop of the South and because it was not harvested until October, property taxes are due on October 31, and considered delinquent on December 31. The poll tax, which was very small in expense, was charged at the polls before casting one's vote. But one was required to have all taxes paid in full before voting, including property taxes. Since the traditional voting date is in early November, many would go to the polls having been unable to pay their property taxes because the cotton crop had not been fully harvested.

Since permission to vote was at the discretion of the polling officials, some white voters would be allowed to vote though they had not paid all their taxes. On the other hand, black voters could be disenfranchised at the polling place for not having their taxes paid in full. This system placed most black voters at a decidedly disadvantaged position as to political power.

If the poll tax failed to disqualify the black voter, a poll test was administered to determine the competency of the voter's ability to vote. These tests required one to answer complicated questions about American governance and eliminated the opportunity for many black voters to actually cast a ballot. Together, the poll tax and poll tests became effective ways of disenfranchising black voters.

In addition to these two laws, a doctrine of "separate but equal" was instituted to separate whites from blacks. This segregationist approach to races included schools, railway accommodations, and various public facilities. The first challenge to this institutionalized segregation was the landmark *Plessy v. Ferguson* case that received its final ruling in the Supreme Court of the United States. In that ruling, the Supreme Court held "separate but equal" to be constitutional and institutionalized segregation for another 65 years.

Jim Crow Laws were a backlash to the harsh treatment Southerners received during the Reconstruction years. Southerners harbored resentments for disenfranchisement, property confiscation, unscrupulous governing agencies, and the federal government intrusion in general. Home rule provided the mechanism for Southern legislatures to settle the score. Poll taxes, poll tests, and segregation were the manifestations of that resentment. What has historically been considered as racist is in fact a reaction to federal oppression. The sons and grandsons of those who survived the brutal treatment during reconstruction could explain their positions well. But by 1920, this resentment born out in segregation and disenfranchisement had morphed into racist hatred. One should remember that there is a great deal of difference in the retribution for injustices and hatred because of the color of one's skin. A closer look at the Ku Klux Klan of 1867 and the KKK of 1920 reveals very different actors motivated be very different causes. To understand culture, it is important to try to understand the motivations behind the actions.

Chapter 5 Sources Used

Arnstein, Robert. *The Trent Affair*. New York: W.W. Norton & Co., 2001.

Berlin, Ira, et al., *Free at Last*. New York: The New York Press, 1992.

Cheek, H. Lee, Jr. *John C. Calhoun Selected Writings and Speeches*. Washington, D.C.: Regnery Publishing, 2003.

DiLorenzo, Thomas J. *The Real Lincoln*. Roseville, CA: Random House, 2002.

Divine, Robert A., et al. *America, Past and Present*. New York: Harper Collins, 1994.

Donald, David. *Lincoln Revisited*. New York: Random House, 1956.

Donald, David. *We Are Lincoln Men*. New York: Simon and Schuster, 2003.

Jones, Howard. *Union in Peril*. Chapel Hill: University of North Carolina Press, 1992.

Kaufman, Michael W. *American Brutus*. New York: Random House, 2004.

Litwack, Leon F. *Been in the Storm Too Long: The Aftermath of Slavery*. New York: Alfred A Knopf, 1979.

Potter, David M. *Lincoln and His Party in the Secession Crisis*. New Haven: Yale University Press, 1948.

Schoenhart-Bailey, Teresa. *British Economic Policy in the 19th Century*. Cambridge: Oxford Press, 1997.

Schweikert, Larry, and Allen, Michael A. *A Patriot's History of the United States*. New York: Sentinel Press, 2004.

Taylor, William R. *Cavalier and Yankee: The Old South and the American National Character*. New York: Harper and Row, 1969.

Tindall, George Brown, and Shi, David Emory. *America: A Narrative History*, 7th ed. New York: W.W. Norton, 2001.

Woodward, C. Van. *The Burden of Southern History.* Baton Rouge: Louisiana State
University Press, 1993.

CHAPTER 6-

The Industrialization of America

Objectives
1. List the names of those who contributed most to industrial growth in America.
2. Explain the moral injustices that arose out of the massive increase in economic power.
3. Describe the moral impulse that led to reform.
4. Describe the Populist Movement and its accomplishments.
5. Describe the Progressive Movement and its accomplishments
6. Explain how the characteristics of the Social Movements of the Second Great Awakening are manifested in the Populist and Progressive Movements.

The four decades following the War Between the States saw millions of European immigrants flood into America. They were coming to America to take advantage of the opportunities that a growing and rapidly industrializing nation afforded. In America they found bustling cities, vast countryside farms, and an unending demand for labor.

Among those who came was a thirteen year old boy named Andrew Carnegie. He went to work with the rest of his family at a sewing factory. He began as a bobbin boy and changed the bobbins on the machines 12 hours per day, six days per week. As he matured he began to inquire of higher wage jobs at every opportunity. His determination led the way for him to work as a telegram delivery boy. In that role he learned to translate the telegraph simply by listening, without having to write the code and decipher it. This skill landed him a job as a telegraph operator. Honing those skills attracted the notice of the president of the Pennsylvania Railroad Company, from whom he learned everything there was to know about railroads because he sent and received every telegram that went through the office.

It became clear to Carnegie that the rapid growth in railroads to accommodate the transport of goods to Eastern markets would require extensive expansion in steel production and bridge construction. To that end, he started the Keystone Bridge Company and began to build the Bridges and produce the rails for expansion. Not only did Carnegie integrate his business horizontally, but he vertically integrated the business as well. He created the most efficient and most tightly controlled vertically integrated business in the world. He drove the price of steel down worldwide by 95% and made the United States the largest steel producing nation in the world.

When Carnegie was a very young man, an acquaintance of Carnegie's would open his personal library of 400 volumes to working boys each Saturday night. Carnegie purposed that if he was ever capable of doing so, he would make sure books were available to any who sought to read them. Such kindnesses influenced Carnegie greatly and may be partly responsible for his philanthropic spirit. When Carnegie sold his business to J. P. Morgan in 1901, it was the largest financial transaction in history to that date. His philanthropic pursuits are still evident today in library funding and the performing arts.

Morgan used Carnegie's company to advance an even greater American industrial effort when he created U.S. Steel Corporation with the acquisition. Morgan's history was quite different as compared to Andrew Carnegie. Morgan was wealthy and was reared in a wealthy family. His Progressive tendencies were focused on efficiency and modernization. As a financier and banker, he was responsible for many mergers of companies, which formed even more efficiencies and economies of scale. His entrepreneurial exploits included the merging of Edison General Electric and Thompson-Houston Electric Company to create General Electric, and he was instrumental in creating U.S. Steel, International Harvester, and AT&T.

J.P. Morgan is credited with forming a coalition of banks to avert the potential catastrophe of the panic of 1893 and then again in 1907. His efforts and the desire to avoid similar crises in the future laid the groundwork for the Federal Reserve Act of 1913 that created the Federal Reserve System. It is but one of the ways in which the Progressive Movement was able to accomplish its goal of fundamentally changing American government.

John D. Rockefeller was the wealthiest man in modern history, boasting a wealth of over $400 billion dollars in present dollar terms. He was the founder of the Standard Oil Company. He was also responsible for consolidating numerous small oil refineries. These consolidations insured the greatest level of efficiencies and economies of scale in the industry. The network of refineries and distribution of petroleum products he created put Standard Oil Company in control of over 90% of the U.S. oil and refined products.

Carnegie, Morgan, and Rockefeller all had a very similar quality about them ... they were visionary. They were able to imagine what great strides in industry could be accomplished with the abundance of natural resources, an abundance of labor (provided mostly by immigrants), and available capital for expansion. These men and others catapulted the United States to the forefront of industrial nations and produced the most inexpensive of products because of the great efficiencies attained. Although their accomplishments were massive and transformative for the nation, there were many problems and injustices that accompanied the success.

Massive immigration to the United States between 1860 and 1910, in excess of 40 million by some estimates, brought an abundance of cheap labor to the United States. While that sort of labor pool was beneficial to industry, cities became overcrowded, leading to slum conditions in many large cities, disease plagued urban populaces, unfair wages paid, child labor proliferated, and food and water quality standards that were abysmal. Further, the power of railroads and big capital squeezed the profits of farms and rural areas across the country by imposing high rates for the storage of grains at railheads and the rates for transporting crops to markets. Because of the high tariffs on foreign imported goods, which benefited American manufacturing concerns, higher prices could be charged by domestic firms, further cutting into profits on American farms.

On both the rural front among the nation's farmers and in the cities among immigrant labor populations, two movements, emerging from separate moral impulses, brought pressure to bear on the political and social climate of the nation. Their emergence was in response to critical injustices that were threatening the very ideals which Americans espoused. History refers to them as the Populists and Progressives.

The Populist Movement was a response to the injustices which plagued America's farming communities. In 1866, the Grange movement within the Populist movement began its work to reduce rail and storage rates and expanded to include the creation of farmer's cooperatives. By 1875, the Grange boasted membership exceeding 857,000 men and women. By working together, farmers could buy supplies and materials at a lower price because of the power of a collective purchase. Further, by combining their crops to lower storage prices, they were able to realize profits that up until that point were going to the railroads.

Their efforts didn't just stop at the economic cooperative emphasis, but also included political action to address the hardships caused by year on year indebtedness, weather related setbacks, and declining drop prices. By 1892, Populists created the People's Party. The party platform called for free coinage of silver currency to inflate the prices of farm commodities, a progressive income tax on the wealthiest Americans, an eight hour work day, and controlled immigration to protect American jobs. The election of 1892 yielded ten congressmen, five senators, and the highest vote count in American history for a third party candidate.

Progressives sought to reform and control the burgeoning American capitalist surge. It was never their intent to destroy capitalism in America. To the Progressive, politics was a struggle between that which was good and that which was evil. It was a war, a religious war, executed against corruption in government and in business. At the center of the Progressive movement was a philosophical shift from traditional methods to modernized methods. This was emphasized as useful in business as well as government. Businesses, in the estimation of the Progressives, had to become more honest and safe. Additionally, government had to become efficient and responsive to the needs of society.

Progressivism found fertile ground in both men and women, democrats and republicans, labor unions and business executives, farmers and rural populations, and almost every demographic in the country. It was the goal of the Progressives to "fundamentally change American government." And that they did, by harnessing the efforts of novelists and newspaper men to aggressively educate the public about the injustices and wrongdoing of both government and business.

Teddy Roosevelt called these journalistic crusaders "muckrakers." These men wrote of the terrible slum conditions of New York and Chicago, the unsanitary food processing conditions, and municipal corruption. Together, the Progressives and their "muckrakers" sought to approach all issues with an overarching virtue of elevating the public interest over that of private greed. Because many Progressives were motivated by religious belief, most of their focus was on moral reform, and they sought to use government as an agency of human welfare.

The Classical Progressive Movement lasted from about 1890 until the end of the First World War. It reflected a concern for the state of society and a conviction that human compassion and scientific investigation could bring problems to light and solve them. It sought the expansion of the government's role and authority in accomplishing the Progressive goals. They were ardent supporters of regulations to break up trusts and monopolies in order to create more competition among industry groups. These social activists desired to see a level of morality legislated through the prohibition of alcohol, child labor laws, and the establishment of Sunday closing laws or "blue laws." And they sought to create a better democracy through primaries and direct election of senators.

As a university president in the 1880s, President Woodrow Wilson spoke to the idea of an administrative state, populated by experts that made efficient, effective use of government on behalf of the people. As President, his idea of a "New Freedom" envisioned a federal government that restored competition and gave the control and administration of social programs to the states, not one that just regulated monopolies. His election restored power to the Democratic Party for the first time since the War Between the States.

During his presidency, Wilson lowered the tariffs on imported goods and pushed through the Federal Reserve Act that placed banks under the regulation of the federal government. Most transformative though was the ratification of four amendments to the Constitution of the United States that "fundamentally changed American government." These amendments reflect the Progressive cause (16th amendment-National Income Tax, 17th amendment-Direct Election of Senators, 18th amendment-prohibition of alcohol, and the 19th amendment-Women's Voting Rights). In these amendments, one can see the ongoing thread of social movement which had its roots in the Great Awakenings of the 18th and 19th century Abolition (Direct Election of Senators), Temperance (prohibition of alcohol), and Suffrage (Women's Right to Vote).

Progressivism, while speaking to greater democracy, did little to strengthen black voting rights or the rights of immigrants. It was a movement of an emerging middle class in America and often excluded the poor from having a voice in its politics. It also brought to light a growing Socialist element in the United States that continued to grow after the Progressives' hey days were passed.

Chapter 6 Sources Used

Divine, Robert A., et al. *America, Past and Present.* New York: Harper Collins, 1994.

Graff, Henry F. *Grover Cleveland.* New York: Henry Holt and Company, 2002.

Morris, Edmund. *Theodore Rex.* New York: Random House, 2001.

Mowry, George E. *The Era of Theodore Roosevelt and the birth of Modern America 1900-1912.* New York: Harper and Row, 1962.

Roosevelt, Theodore Louis Auchincloss, ed. *Letters and Speeches of Theodore Roosevelt.* New York: Literary Classics, 2004.

Schweikert, Larry and Allen, Michael A. *A Patriot's History of the United States.* New York: Sentinel Press, 2004.

Tindall, George Brown, and Shi, David Emory. *America: A Narrative History, 7th ed.* New York: W.W. Norton, 2007.

CHAPTER 7-

Traditionalism, Modernism, and the Moral Navigation in Poverty and Plenty

Objectives
1. Distinguish the differences in Traditionalism, Modernism, Evangelicalism, and Fundamentalism.
2. Describe the differences in the Symptoms and the Causes of the Great Depression.
3. Explain the differences in those who believed government intervention during economic crisis is necessary versus those who believe it to be immoral and unconstitutional.
4. Explain the concept of American Exceptionalism.

How does a nation navigate rapidly changing social norms when the traditional approaches to social issues, based on Judeo-Christian principles, are challenged by science and modernistic approaches to social issues? At the turn of the 20th century, Traditionalism came under ever increasing pressure to demonstrate scientifically proof of truths that had been accepted for centuries. Among these changing perspectives were a woman's acceptable role in society, Creationism versus Darwinism, government's role in the lives of people, and the eternal nature of the human soul and the ramifications that might have on one's behavior in society.

Traditionalism is political and religious philosophy that asserts liberty is only secured by the rule of law. Law then, as a social contract between man and the government man creates, sets limits as to the domain in which man functions independently of government and the domain within which government secures the liberties of man. This position is premised on the concept of natural law and that a rational man is governed by his own conscience and requires no government except that which protects him from irrational man.

The traditionalist believes that religious beliefs and traditional social norms inform the conscience of man and reinforce his behavior within society. Further, they believe that a transcendent moral order exists, rooted in the Holy Scriptures of the

Bible, and that this order is confirmed in nature (clock-like mechanism of the planets, orderly changing of the seasons, the precision of the coming of day and night, etc.).

Modernism is based on three assumptions: (1) God does not exist; (2) In view of the horrors World War I and its aftermath, reality is a human construction that is not necessarily rational or orderly; (3) Social progress does not occur organically, it is created. These assumptions placed Modernism in diametric opposition to Traditionalism. Among the most recognizable Modernists were Albert Einstein, whose theory of relativity opened the door to a reality that was not based on observation or objectivity, and Sigmund Freud, who asserted that one's reality may not be observable to another because human reality is a subjective experience and is very personal.

It is impossible to overstate the causal effect of World War I on the social concept of modernist reality. The underpinnings of Western Civilization were shaken by the "Great War," and those young men who came of age in the horrors of it were said to be a "lost generation." The optimistic idealism of that generation dissolved into a deeply pessimistic cynicism. As Hemingway posited in *Farewell to Arms*, "abstract words such as glory, honor, and courage" have become obscene.

Modern science made war more deadly than ever before in history. The magnitude of those losses, witnessed by those who would survive, left those survivors with the disturbing conclusions that "all Gods (are) dead, all wars fought, and all faiths in man shaken." Gertrude Stein, in a conversation with Ernest Hemingway, speaking of those who had endured the war declared, "You are (lost). You have no respect for anything. You drink yourselves to death." Modern science had made things more efficient and effective, but in the thinking of the modernists, it left those of 1920s and 1930s despairing of hope as to their purpose and without answers to the growing complexities of the world.

The Modernist of the 1920s is best demonstrated in the work of F. Scott Fitzgerald. Through his novels he made his readers aware of the "self-indulgent and self-destructive people who drank too much and partied too much." The prosperity of the 1920s brought an opportunity for the Modernist to engage in reckless behavior as both a tranquilizer to the remembrances of the past and an escape from the realities of the present. The painful realities of the "Great War" morphed into the devastating reality of a global economic crisis beginning in the late 1920s and lasting through 1946.

Amidst this backdrop, in perhaps the most defining controversy between Traditionalists and Modernists, Creationism was challenged by Darwinism, and the grand debate was borne out in the Scopes Monkey Trial. Darwinism disputed the long held Creationists' belief in a creator, God, who made the Earth and all that is in it in six days, resting on the seventh. Darwinism claimed that all that life originated from a single species. Over time, through adaptation and natural selection, all species evolved into their present day form. Natural selection asserted a "survival of the fittest" principle to explain how some species failed to adapt and by nature ceased to exist.

The State of Tennessee legislature outlawed the teaching of Darwinism in public schools and colleges in 1925. John T. Scopes, a substitute teacher in Dayton, Tennessee became the challenge case against the new state law. The trial drew international attention and brought hundreds of people to the small Tennessee town. The defense for Scopes came from Clarence Darrow, who was arguably the most well-known defense attorney in the nation. The prosecution's expert witness was William Jennings Bryan, a former Democratic candidate for President of the United States.

The trial challenged Creationism's believability on the basis of some of the rather incredible stories found in the Bible, such as the Great Flood, Jonah's experience in the belly of a fish, and Eve's creation from the rib of Adam. The defense did not seek acquittal of Scopes on the culpability of his having taught evolutionism. It sought to compel people of faith to at least consider that there may be explanations for the origins of life other than simply that which is found in the Bible. To the Traditionalist they are mutually exclusive. To admit one to be plausible dismisses the plausibility of the other.

The Scopes trial is perhaps the dividing line between an America steadfast in its traditionalism and the America that would emerge more open to other explanations. The greatest test of Modernism and Traditionalism would be finding hope in the midst of the economic calamity we call the "Great Depression." With problems so complex, it strained the intellect and the soul for solutions.

Perhaps one of the most misunderstood characteristics of the period from 1927-1933 is distinguishing the differences between the causes and the symptoms of the "Great Depression." Too many in America today the Great Depression was caused by the October 29, 1929, stock market crash. However, the stock market crash was only a symptom of the Great Depression. The causes can be seen in a number of things in the 1920s which caused the era to devastate so many. The near apocalyptical nature of World War I created numerous conditions which made the Great Depression more severe than it might have been otherwise.

World War I created an economic boom for the United States. War material and supplies produced for Great Britain and France propelled the United States past rival industrial nations and created jobs that improved the lives of most Americans. When the war ended, the production capacity remained and fed a growing demand for manufactured goods domestically and abroad.

Innovations in household appliances drove a demand from women who desired to make homemaking more efficient and provide more time for other pursuits. Radio sales soared as broadcasting systems brought news and entertainment from all over the world. Electricity augmented the demand for new appliances and technology, making the conveniences more and more attractive to eager consumers. By 1926, the capacity to produce reached an all-time high, and it seemed as though there was no end in sight for the consumer demand.

The introduction of consumer credit, beginning with the General Motors Acceptance Corporation, made everything from radios to automobiles affordable to the average citizen. This type of installment payment system allowed the consumer to own appliances, automobiles, etc. with very little paid down and then monthly payments till the contract was complete. With ease of purchase, consumer demand for manufactured goods soared. But so did the consumer's debt. Consumer debt and overproduction of manufactured goods worked hand in hand, and in part caused the Great Depression.

When it became evident in 1927 that inventory levels were rising and sales were slowing, manufacturers began to reduce output and eventually reduced personnel. As layoffs began to increase, so did the default on consumer debt. It would, however, be another two years before the reality of the decline would be manifested. By that time, the spiral had already begun its downward trajectory.

In a very similar way, Americans began to invest in the stock markets and to invest in the market using margin loans. Margin loans gave the investor the ability to buy stocks by paying only a fraction of the market value of the stock but being able to profit on any appreciation in the price of the stock purchased. And in the 1920s people were investing with money they couldn't afford through broker or margin loans. The rest of the world's markets depended on the U.S. market conditions. To the seasoned broker, the U.S. stock market was manifesting high price to earnings ratios. To make matters even more financially dangerous, margin requirements were very loose. In other words, brokers required investors to put in very little of their own money. Today, the Federal Reserve requires margin debts be limited to 50 percent. But during the 1920s, debts were allowed up to 90 percent of the value of the stock purchased.

When the industrial producers began to cut production and reduce their labor force, stock values began to decline as well. By October 1929, America had over-produced, over-speculated, and acquired much more debt than they should have. The stock market crash of October 29, 1929, was one of the first symptoms that the United States was facing a Great Depression.

By 1932, the United States was facing a 25% unemployment rate with large cities facing unemployment rates in excess of 50%. Those who still worked had both hours and wages reduced. The rural communities where farmers had not enjoyed the prosperity of the rest of the country were hit especially hard by the crisis. In a matter of months, 500,000 Americans lost their homes or farms to mortgage foreclosure. Things worsened in 1933 with over 4,000 banks closing in the first quarter alone, erasing over $3.6 billion in deposits of working class families.

In Europe, with a populous still reeling from World War I, the financial calamity in the United States sent shock waves across the continent. Among a people stunned by both crises, Modernism found a home in totalitarian regimes. Adolf Hitler, a dictator fed in his philosophies by Friedrich Nietzsche, provided hope to Germans by advancing a narrative of Germany as a superior race of people and of the *ubermensch* who would lead them. These ubermensch would be above morality and traditional norms.

In America, Traditionalism found a home in evangelicalism and fundamentalism. That which Nietzsche described as superstition onto which man clings in crisis was found to be the salve which made the Great Depression bearable and totalitarianism less likely to blossom. The evangelical message of such preachers as Billy Sunday intertwined patriotism with Christianity. His was a message of hope and spoke to the idea of the moral cleanliness of real manliness. In contrast to the secular nature of Europe, he called Americans back to traditional Christian morality. Once in describing hell, he said, "if you turn hell upside down, you will find 'Made in Germany' stamped on the bottom." Fundamentalism reminded Americans that the world was in its current position because of modernism's assault on all things religious and traditional. In their estimation, modernism and the abandonment of God had led America down a dark path which required a long and difficult return back to faith. The defining difference between the evangelical and the fundamentalist was in the evangelicals' reliance on the saving grace of Jesus freely given to all who would believe. On the other hand, the fundamentalist preached a message of the reality of hell and the surety that one could not inherit heaven if one did not abide closely to the inerrant precepts of the Holy Scripture.

When the Roosevelt administration began to propose various government programs to alleviate the suffering of the American people, traditionalists and modernists clashed over whether or not government should have such a large role in the personal lives of its citizenry. Often the political message misused absolutes in order to convince a Christian populace that they should approve of government's desire to interject in social problems. An absolute is a word that loses its important meaning when modified. But because the political message used a Christian vocabulary and language, it was effective in bringing about a political end. An example of an absolute truth losing its meaning is the word justice. If one modifies the word justice, it takes on a completely different meaning. One is either experiencing justice or one is experiencing a lack of justice. So then a term such as "social justice" has abandoned the meaning of justice and is speaking of either charity or mercy.

From a Christian perspective however, there were reasons that would compel the Christian to reject Roosevelt's intervention programs. They believed God helps those who help themselves and that to engage in such programs was a poor stewarding of the money God had blessed them with. However, there were others who believed that the teachings of Jesus compelled them to take care of "the least of these." (Matthew 25:31-46). To them this was the Christian ideal of charity and mercy.

Some of the programs Franklin Roosevelt put in place to ease the suffering of the American populace during the Great Depression included declaring a bank holiday, then reopening the banks, and establishing several infrastructure programs to improve the unemployment problem. The debate over the morality and constitutionality of the programs would last throughout the Roosevelt administrations terms in office.

Throughout the Great Depression there resonated a sense of patriotism amidst the uncertainty and apparent hopelessness that seemed to veil the nation. It is rooted in the concept of American Exceptionalism. It is credited to Alexis de Tocqueville's observations which led to his writing *Democracy in America*. He said,

---

The position of the Americans is therefore quite exceptional, and it may be believed that no democratic people will ever be placed in a similar one. Their strictly Puritanical origin, their exclusively commercial habits, even the country they inhabit, which seems to divert their minds from the pursuit of science, literature, and the arts, the proximity of Europe, which allows them to neglect these pursuits without relapsing into barbarism, a thousand special causes, of which I have only been able to point out the most important, have singularly concurred to fix the mind of the American upon purely practical objects. His passions, his wants, his education, and religion alone bids him turn, from time to time a transient and distracted glance to heaven. Let us cease, then, to view all democratic nations under the example of the American people.

He theorizes that the United States is "qualitatively different" from other nations. In this view, America's exceptionalism stems from its emergence from a revolution, becoming what political scientist Seymour Martin Lipset called "the first new nation" and developing a uniquely American ideology, "Americanism," based on liberty, egalitarianism, individualism, republicanism, populism, and laissez-faire. This ideology itself is often referred to as "American Exceptionalism."

Chapter 7 Sources Used

Di Lorenzo, Thomas J. *How Capitalism Saved America*. New York: Crown Forum, 2004.

Schweikert, Larry, and Allen, Michael. *A Patriot's History of the United States*. New York: Sentinel Press, 2004.

Marsden, George M. *Religion and American Culture*. Belmont, CA: Cengage Learning, 2001.

Shi, David E., and Tindall, George B. *America: A Narrative History*. New York: W.W. Norton & Co., 2016.

Tocqueville, Alexis de, *Democracy in America*. Chicago: University of Chicago Press, 2000.

Worst Stock Market Crashes. *Stock Brokers and Margin Loans in the 1920's.* (http://www.worststockmarketcrashes.com/stock-market-crashes/stock-brokers-and-margin-loans-in-the-1920s/)

CHAPTER 8-

War, Social Upheaval of the Sixties and Seventies, and Modern American Culture

Objectives
1. Describe America's emergence from the Great Depression to World Power
2. Explain the moral inconsistencies that led to social upheaval
3. Describe the effect of television on American culture
4. Explain the major issues of the 1968 Presidential Election
5. Define Conservatism and Liberalism.

America was catapulted from the grasp of the Great Depression by a global war that it tried desperately to avoid. But it was not to be. World War II did two things for America that perhaps could not have occurred without her entry into the war. First, the war effort mobilized millions of Americans back to work in factories that were producing at only a fraction of their capacity at the outbreak of the war, and that capacity increased over the four years America was involved in the war. Second, by war's end not only was the United States the leading manufacturing nation in nearly every category, but America would also be producing nearly 50% of the world's total manufacturing output for nearly a decade following the war. The war's end though revealed a number of social fault lines that had been masked by the intense focus on the war effort.

The same moral impulses which were behind the abolition, temperance, and the suffrage movement would reemerge in the civil rights movement, the anti-drug movement, and the women's rights movement. It was through these grass roots efforts that social change would again take priority in the public mind. The movements reflected the same struggle to grasp the lofty ideals set forth in the Declaration of Independence; ideals and values that have been set so high that they may never be reached, but that have nonetheless perpetuated an America restless for greater liberty.

Men returning from war found their jobs filled by women and minorities. And some men of color found that the service they had rendered to save democracy abroad was not fully appreciated in their own country. Although the American military had been desegregated following the War Between the States, President Woodrow Wilson segregated the military by executive order during World War I. Some thirty years later President Harry Truman desegregated the military again following World War II. The moral inconsistencies that were obvious to anyone watching ignited the moral impulse for change.

At the heart of the civil rights movement was a desire to see segregation end. This latent discontent came to full maturity in the face of the paradox of returning soldiers of color being treated unequally in the very nation for which they had sacrificed to serve. These men were segregated and discriminated against in the workplace, in restaurants, with travel accommodations, and public transportation. Even their children were segregated in the schools they attended.

President Truman's desegregation executive order set of a firestorm in the Democratic Party. It even split the party in the 1948 presidential election to the extent that a splintered party offshoot, the Dixiecrats, ran an opposing candidate against Truman in that election. This discontent brought national exposure to an issue long overdue for resolve. It was a constitutional issue to most. Could a nation, built on freedom and the equality of man, create a lower class of citizen to which it would not afford the blessings of liberty afforded to others?

Segregation found its strength for perpetuation in the 1896 Supreme Court ruling in *Plessy v. Ferguson* for over 50 years. The ruling had upheld state laws sanctioning segregation. *Plessy v Ferguson* came under assault though in 1954 when the constitutionality of another state law was tested in the Supreme Court. In *Brown v. Board of Education*, the Supreme Court essentially overturned *Plessy v. Ferguson*, when it ruled 9-0 in favor of the plaintiff challenging the constitutionality of segregation in public schools. This landmark case and its implementation brought about tremendous social upheaval and revealed long-held, deep-seated resentments against the federal government and against black Americans seeking equal treatment under the law. It also reawakened old bitterness toward federal intervention to upend states' rights to govern themselves. This bitterness was best reflected in clashes at Little Rock High School in Little Rock, Arkansas. Later a similar occurrence took place at the University of Alabama. (See also this you tube link "A Confrontation for Integration at the University of Alabama") As one may ascertain by viewing the films of the days following the ruling, at the center of the upheaval was a clash between 10th amendment rights of states to govern themselves without federal intervention into state matters and the 14th amendment rights of minorities to enjoy equal protection under the law as guaranteed by the constitution.

Desegregation of public transportation received national attention when, on December 1, 1955, a black woman, Rosa Parks, refused to yield her seat on a city bus to a white man in Montgomery, Alabama. Parks was arrested and became the catalyst for the Montgomery Bus Boycott. The boycott was organized by many of the civil rights leaders in Montgomery including Martin Luther King, Jr., Rosa Parks, E.D. Nixon, and others. For over a year, black residents of Montgomery refused to ride the city buses and found transportation through carpooling and walking. The boycott came to an end when the financial pressure mounted for the bus service whose primary patrons were black. By 1956, the Supreme Court ruled that the segregation policies of Montgomery's bus service were unconstitutional. As a result of the boycott, Dr. Martin Luther King, Jr. and Rosa Parks became nationally known figures in the civil rights movement.

Dr. Martin Luther King, Jr. led a civil rights march to Washington, D.C. in August 1963 that culminated in his most famous public address. On the steps of the Lincoln Memorial, King declared that he and those there with him had come to redeem a promissory note that had been returned to black Americans marked "NSF." He advanced a "dream" that he had. King's dream was of an America where all its citizens enjoyed the same freedoms regardless of color. His success could be seen in the way that his supporters met violence with non-violent responses. King's home was bombed, but he remained steadfast in his commitment to non-violence. Many who rode public buses in protests were beaten but met the violence with continued non-violent protest. Churches were bombed, individuals murdered, police dogs unleashed on protesters, and fire hoses turned on those who demanded equal treatment under the law.

President Kennedy had given much lip service to the movement, but as of King's "I Have a Dream" speech in August 1963 he had not introduced substantive legislation to make the real changes desired by the movement. Perhaps the delays were associated with other concerns facing the nation at the time. Kennedy's election marked a sharp political shift in America. His focus in the 1960 campaign had been on domestic reform and foreign advancement. Domestic reform has remained somewhat stalled in the midst of three important international events of significance to national security.

First, the conflict in Vietnam between the democratic forces of South Vietnam and the communist forces of North Vietnam became significant because of Defense and State department concerns which were called the Domino Theory. Domino theory asserted that if Democratic South Vietnam fell to communism, the rest of Southeast Asia would likely fall to communism like dominoes. The Kennedy administration believed that material prosperity would go far in eventually winning the "hearts and minds" of the Vietnamese people. An initiative for General Economic Progress was launched by the Kennedy administration and was eventually supported by American troops in Vietnam. By mid-1963 Kennedy had ordered 17,000 American troops to the area.

To complicate Kennedy's efforts in Vietnam, President Diem, the democratically elected leader of South Vietnam, began an open persecution of Buddhists in South Vietnam. As an ally of the United States, Diem was asked by President Kennedy to cease his distasteful practices because it created a very poor public relations image for South Vietnam and the United States. President Diem was Catholic and had cracked down on practicing Buddhists by banning the flying of the traditional Buddhist flag prohibiting Buddhists from exercising the same religious freedoms as Catholics, and the continued detainment of Buddhist monks and nuns. Buddhist monks had begun public protests of Diem's policies by self-immolation. These acts of protests had brought much negative attention to the nation.

When Diem persisted in his ill treatment of Buddhists, Kennedy ordered CIA operatives to take Diem into custody and remove him from office so that a leader could be installed with a more democratic approach to religious liberties in Vietnam. The detention of Diem went wrong when elements of opposition to Diem assassinated him while in CIA custody, creating an international embarrassment for a democratic cause in South Vietnam.

Second, Cuban nationals long grieved by the overthrow of their government by Fidel Castro sought to take back their nation and oust Castro from power. These Cubans, along with elements of the CIA, developed a planned invasion designed to reestablish a democratic government in Cuba. The plan was approved by Kennedy himself. However, even as the invasion into Cuba's Bay of Pigs was under way, Kennedy withdrew American support abruptly, leaving the Cubans to the mercy of the Castro government. This act instilled an attitude of hatred toward Kennedy by both Fidel Castro and the Cuban nationals in the United States and alerted the Cuban government to the possibility of future American aggression toward Cuba.

Third, Nikita Khrushchev of the Soviet Union authorized the building of the Berlin Wall, segregating communist East Germany from democratic West Germany. The building of the wall met a non-response from Kennedy. This emboldened Khrushchev to place nuclear weapons in Cuba. For two weeks following the discovery of the weapons on the island by American reconnaissance planes, the United States was on the brink of war with the Soviet Union. Not until a naval quarantine was imposed on Cuba did the Soviets agree to remove the weapons.

By November 1963, Kennedy was facing pressures on both the international and domestic levels to solve growing crises. It was in this atmosphere of discontent that Kennedy made a campaign trip to Dallas, Texas to begin shoring up his support for the upcoming 1964 presidential election. It was during that trip that President Kennedy was assassinated while riding in a convertible through downtown Dallas. Shocked, the nation sought those responsible for the killing. The list of suspects was long: Fidel Castro's Cuba, Nikita Khrushchev's Soviet Union, the mafia that had help elect him and whom he had the justice department investigate, right wing Cuban exiles still angered over the Bay of Pigs fiasco, and Lee Harvey Oswald.

Conspiracy theories abound even today about how and who was responsible for the death of the president. In the end, Lee Harvey Oswald was the accused killer. Before he could be tried, he was killed while in transit from the Dallas City jail to his arraignment by Jack Ruby. Oswald's death effectively ended the investigation and settled the case.

On every front, at the end of 1963, the United States was facing real potential upheaval. A large part of the nation still believed that Kennedy had been elected by suspicious means, a cloud of secrecy still hung over the assassination of the president, the isolation of the military from planning strategy in Vietnam had gotten the effort in Southeast Asia off to a rocky and suspicious start, President Diem's assassination still loomed in the recent past, and civil rights legislation that had been long delayed by the president was still awaiting introduction to Congress.

Beginning in 1964, in rapid succession the Congress enacted the 1964 Civil Rights Act and the 1965 Voting Rights Act. These actions of Congress occurred in the midst of some of the most vicious attacks on volunteers seeking to register voters in Mississippi and Alabama for the upcoming 1964 election. What became known as Freedom Summer was very dangerous time for those seeking to extend the power of the vote to those who had been intimidated into disenfranchisement. The 1965 Voting Rights Act came on the heels of the Selma-Montgomery March demanding voting rights.

A change in focus was made to the civil rights movement after the Voting Rights Act was passed. The new emphasis was on cities in the North plagued by poverty, urban blight, and de facto segregation. In particular, Chicago and Detroit became the focal points for urban renewal and equal housing rights. Then with Memphis sanitation workers on strike, Dr. King went to Memphis to draw attention to the unfair wages of sanitation workers. King had accomplished much since 1955. He secured a plan for desegregation, achieved in getting a civil rights act passed, gained a voting rights act, and outlawed poll taxes and poll tests via constitutional amendments. His remarks in Memphis, from the balcony of the Lorraine Motel on April 4, 1968, seem prophetic today. Perhaps in this final speech, *I've Been To The Mountaintop*, he was reflecting upon all that had been accomplished and that was still left to be accomplished. Moments after the speech he was shot in the face by an assassin.

The death of King brought an end to non-violent protest and an end to the Classical Civil Rights Movement. It came in the middle of the 1968 Presidential Election.

The 1968 election reflected the growing discontent of the country and was seen in three very important campaign issues: the Vietnam War, Civil Rights, and Poverty. The leading democrat party candidates were Hubert Humphrey, Eugene McCarthy and

Robert Kennedy. The Democratic National Convention was sure to be rife with demonstrations because of remaining unfulfilled promises addressing civil rights and the ongoing discontent over the Vietnam War. The non-violent civil rights movement was no longer non-violent or civil. And radicals and anti-war liberals grew increasing more violent in their protests in 1968.

The primary elections for nomination of the democrat party had Hubert Humphrey in the lead with the second place candidates reasonably close, with a slight edge to Eugene McCarthy until the California primary. When Kennedy won that primary, it made the race potentially much closer. Within moments after celebrating the California victory, Robert Kennedy was gunned down by an assassin. The shock of the killing prompted McCarthy to suspend his

Campaign, and he never returned to it. Although Humphrey won the nomination, the democrat party was damaged by the riots and protests that ensued at the convention that August. And they would lose the election to the republican candidate, Richard Nixon.

It was as though the entire country breathed a sigh of relief when 1968 finally came to an end. The year had begun with the Tet Offensive in the Vietnam War, an all-out, full scale offensive by the Viet Cong of South Vietnam and North Vietnamese Army against the United States forces and South Vietnamese Army forces along many fronts. It was sudden and shocking but ended with decisive victory by the United States and its allies. What made Tet so dramatic socially in the United States was television.

Television's effect on American society cannot be overstated. It brought international and domestic events into the homes of average Americans in real time, and America was able to witness things that previous generations would only have read about in the news days after the events occurred. America witnessed the presidential debates between Kennedy and Nixon, the launching of the first manned flights into space, the assassination of President Kennedy, the assassination of Robert Kennedy, the assassination of Martin Luther King, Jr., the Selma-Montgomery march, race riots, Vietnam war protests, the death of a student protester at Kent State University, and the horror of the Vietnam War including daily broadcasts of the Tet Offensive and the brutal fighting that came with it. It seemed through 1968 that most of the television broadcasts were of tragic, bad news. America saw it all on television. It was no longer in a distant, faraway place; it was in Americans' living rooms.

1969 seemed to bring new hope. The promise by President Kennedy to land a man on the moon and return him safely to the earth before the end of the decade looked as though it might become a reality. The final push toward that goal came in July 1969, when on the 20th of that month, the Apollo 11 mission landed on the moon. America watched it on television. Those grainy, black and white television transmissions kept Americans on the edge of their seats until the commander of the Lunar Module announced, "Houston, this is Tranquility Base. The Eagle has landed." And Americans later witnessed Neil Armstrong moving cautiously down the ladder outside the Lunar Module, stepping onto the surface of the moon and declaring, "One small step for man, one giant leap for mankind!"

The Vietnam War still raged, but hope had once again returned. America needed a victory in 1969 that all Americans could celebrate. President Nixon promised to end the war in Vietnam, and a believing nation trusted that it would happen. In January 1973, after much loss of life and treasure, a cease fire was declared. The cessation in fighting came after a massive bombing campaign in December 1972, a dramatic shift in the U.S. / China foreign policy, and firm talk from a new president. Richard Nixon was committed to ending the war but not abandoning the commitments made to America's allies. It was this commitment that tested America's resolve on the other side of the world that same year. America watched it on television.

In October 1973, Egypt and Syria launched coordinated attacks against Israel to recover territories lost during the 1967 Arab-Israeli War. Both wars were humiliating defeats for the Arab States involved. The steadfast loyalty of the United States in supporting Israel angered

Arab Oil Producing states, and an embargo of oil was imposed on the United States and other Western nations. The embargo quadrupled gasoline prices and crippled the U.S. economy. The effects would continue throughout the decade and made American relations tense with the Middle East for a generation. Americans watched on television the long lines of those awaiting an opportunity to fill their tanks with gasoline.

Richard Nixon won the 1972 reelection as president. The victory was a landslide and reflected the continued hope and confidence the American people had placed in Nixon. The war truly seemed on a trajectory toward a resolve. Tensions between the United States and China seemed to be easing, and America's space program was the envy of the world. But during the summer and fall of 1973, evidence began to mount that the Nixon administration had conspired to cover up a break in at the Democratic National Committee headquarters in the Watergate building in Washington, D.C. It would prove to be the undoing of the Nixon presidency.

Nixon accomplished much as president. But all that he had been able to accomplish for good was overshadowed by the criminal activities and obstruction of justice that his administration had carried out. He was forced to resign the presidency on August 8, 1974 to take effect the next day at noon. He was succeeded by his Vice President, Gerald Ford. President Ford took over a White House that had been crippled by scandal and was in desperate need of restoring the faith and confidence of the nation. America watched it on television.

In the spring of 1975, communist forces of North Vietnam began an offensive which ended with the fall of Saigon, the capital of South Vietnam. Collapse of defensive forces was shocking to both the South Vietnamese and American military officials. By April, it was evident that Saigon could not be defended. Emergency evacuation measures were implemented to remove American diplomatic personnel from the embassy building in Saigon. Armed forces helicopters flew round the clock missions carrying load after load of personnel to ships safely offshore. The heartbreak of many Americans was to witness the many Vietnamese people begging for the opportunity to board one of the many evacuation helicopters. America watched in on television.

The fifteen year period ending in 1975 reflects the most socially impactful era of the twentieth century. By the end of this tumultuous period, four prominent national figures had been assassinated, including a President of the United States and a U.S. Senator, hundreds of thousands were franchised with voting rights, separate but equal was a thing of the past and guaranteed by federal law, over 58,000 Americans had died in Southeast Asia, hundreds had died in race riots in America's largest cities, man had landed on the moon only ten years after the first rockets were launched into space, an attempted assassination was made in the 1972 election, a president was forced to resign for illegal activities, and minority groups not previously heard of began demanding rights under the constitution. The events of the era solidified a growing conservative movement that gained its full momentum in 1980. The era marked the beginning of a distrust of government that would lead to the Reagan Revolution.

Modern liberalism and conservatism can trace their roots to the New Deal Policies of the Franklin Roosevelt administration. However, the lines between conservatism and liberalism were blurred. Those that might have considered themselves liberal in the early days of the Roosevelt administration balked at many of Roosevelt's programs as excessive, frivolous, and wasteful. However, to avoid the appearance of having a lack of compassion for the needy during the difficult years of the Great Depression, they joined forces with the Roosevelt team to alleviate the suffering of the poor and destitute. On the other hand, conservatives that felt the need to provide help to the hurting realized the cost of Roosevelt's programs were terribly expensive to put in place and voted against them to avoid the appearance of irresponsibility.

Liberals see government as an active participant in the lives of Americans with a strong focus on minority rights, government funded programs, regulation of commerce, and active use of the judicial system to correct the social ills which are found difficult to achieve through the legislative process. To accomplish these agendas, liberals support a tax structure, generally opposed by conservatives, that is focused on taxation on those that are most able to pay it.

Conservatives view government as a necessary evil that must be kept in check and reduced in order to free up capital to taxpayers. Conservatives believe that lower taxes stimulate economic growth, and lowering taxes raises revenues that flow into the federal treasury. Conservatives generally put a high value on foreign affairs and a strong military presence to maintain the safety and security of America.

While the lines were blurred between liberal and conservative points of view in the 1930s, they became very distinct in the years directly following the communist takeover of Vietnam and the Presidential Election of 1976. A low voter turnout in 1976 revealed the lost trust in government and the apathy Americans felt about the two lackluster candidates from which they were to choose. What the 1976 election did reveal was the powerful challenge that Ronald Reagan brought to the Republican Party and its less than stellar handling of a number of crises, including the economy, Vietnam, and the Middle East Conflict.

The 1976 Presidential Election was a contest between Republican incumbent President Gerald Ford and Democrat Nominee Governor Jimmy Carter of the state of Georgia. The

Republican Party was still reeling from the political damage inflicted by the Watergate scandal and the resignation of President Richard Nixon. Gerald Ford was an unelected president. Jimmy Carter was an outsider to Washington and brought with him a belief that integrity and honor could once again be restored to the White House.

The election issues centered on the stagnant American economy, the ongoing crisis in the Middle East, and America's dependency on foreign oil. When Jimmy Carter was elected president, he took over a nation struggling to find traction with its economy. The Vietnam War had created a staggering accumulated debt, the abandonment of the Bretton Woods agreement by President Nixon was sure to result in inflation, and oil price increases compounded the problems of both.

The 1979 Iranian Revolution resulted in the ousting of the Shah of Iran, an American ally. Resentments toward the United States because of its support of the Shah were borne out by radicals in the revolution taking the American Embassy staff in Iran hostage. The revolution also created a disruption in the production of oil in Iran and other oil producing nations sending gasoline prices in the United States soaring once again, and Americans again waited in long gas lines for a fill up. For the last two years of the Carter Administration, Americans watched each evening as television networks updated the country on the hostage crisis in Iran and the oil crisis at home. Americans watched as their countrymen were paraded from place to place, blind-folded and bound, and the federal government seemingly powerless to do anything about their plight or the continuing oil shortage.

The first Carter administration came to a close with a disastrous economy, foreign policy failures, blunders in an attempt to rescue embassy hostages, and a lack of ability to lead the American people in a time of crisis. The liberal policies of the Carter Administration stood in stark contrast to the voice of conservatism in the election of 1980. Ronald Reagan, the republican candidate for president in the 1980 election, contrasted liberalism and conservatism in a way the American public was able to understand. This was in large part a result of Reagan's ability to articulate a conservative policy that not only addressed conservative politics in governmental policy, but tied economy, foreign policy, military strength, government spending, and domestic policy to family values and morality. He attacked liberal policies for weakening military capability, for signaling weak foreign policy, and for perpetuating a stagnant economy beset by inflation and unemployment.

Declaring taxes too high and government too bloated, Reagan promised to unleash the powerful potential of the United States. Reagan spoke of America in glowing and optimistic terms which inspired the populace. It should have been no surprise that his landslide election was an endorsement of optimism over pessimism.

Traditionalism, evangelicalism, and fundamentalism found a home in the conservative movement of 1976-80. The message delivered by Ronald Reagan and others translated into political language that similar morality and Judeo-Christian foundation voices had espoused in the 19th century. To the conservative, there are eternal truths to be found in Judeo-Christian teaching which support the American ideals of liberty, equal justice under the law, the sanctity of life, the sacred nature of marriage, the free will of man, and the concept of an eternal supreme judge.

Modernism, secularism, Nietzscheism, and nihilism found a home in liberalism. Progress is seen as the embracement of new solutions to old problems, even to the abandonment of traditionally and universally held values and morality. Those truths that are held to be eternal, in the estimation of the liberal, are of a religious nature and have no place in the realm of politics or government. To that end then, modernism and traditionalism, conservatism and liberalism, are at odds on many fronts socially, and it has evolved into what some have dubbed a cultural war in America.

Among the oft debated issues in America today are the rights of those who, in the view of the conservative, are trampling upon the rights of others and demanding acceptance disguised as tolerance. Most notable issues are gay / lesbian marriage rights, definition of marriage, late term abortion rights, gender identification, and euthanasia. To the traditionalist conservative, the issues are not debatable because they are governed by eternal truths. All these debates are solved in scripture and are judged by an eternal judge. To the modernist liberal, the issues are debatable because science has either borne them out to be natural or not yet solved.

Dr. Linda Dennard of Auburn University once remarked, "Democracy thrives in ambiguity." In a thriving democracy like ours, the cultural and social debates may just be the engine that makes America what she is. Many will disagree and agree to disagree. No matter the outcome, America remains what it has been since 1607, the place all want to be.

Chapter 8 Sources Used

Blank, Stephen J., et al. *Culture, Conflict and History*. Maxwell Air Force Base: Air University Press, 2002.

Collins, Randall. *The Sociology of Philosophies: A Global Theory of Intellectual Change*. Cambridge: Harvard University Press, 1998.

Herring, George C. *America's Longest War: The United States and Vietnam, 1950-1975*. New York: McGraw Hill, 2002.

Hinman, Ellwood P. *The Politics of Coercion*. Maxwell Air Force Base: Air University Press, 2002.

Jacoby, Susan. *The Age of American Unreason*. New York: Pantheon Books, 2008.

Kissinger, Henry. *Diplomacy*. New York: Simon and Schuster, 1994.

Lane, Mark. *Plausible Denial: Was the CIA Involved in the Assassination of JFK*. New York: Thunder's Mouth Press, 1991.

Schweikert, Larry, and Allen, Michael A. *A Patriot's History of the United States*. New York: Sentinel Press, 2004.

Sugrue, Thomas J. *Sweet Land of Liberty: The Forgotten Struggle for Civil Rights in the North*. New York: Random House, 2008.

Tindall, George Brown, and Shi, David Emory. *America: A Narrative History*, 7th ed. New York: W.W. Norton, 2007.

Warren, Earl. *The Warren Report: The Official Report on the Assassination of President John F. Kennedy*. New York: The Associated Press, 1964.

We the People of the United States, in Order to form a more perfect Union, establish Justice, ensure domestic Tranquility, provide for the common defence, promote the general Welfare, and secure the Blessings of Liberty to ourselves and our Posterity, do ordain and establish this Constitution for the United States of America.